Regina Toedter

# HOLISTAY

## How I travel at home
## to always be on holiday

Publisher: BoD · Books on Demand GmbH, In de Tarpen 42,
22848 Norderstedt, bod@bod.de
Print: Libri Plureos GmbH, Friedensallee 273, 22763 Hamburg
ISBN: 978-3-7693-2290-3

**Bibliographic information of the German National Library:** The German National Library lists this publication in the German National Bibliography; detailed bibliographic data is available on the internet at dnb.d-nb.de.

**Disclaimer:** The advice, tips and recommendations presented in this book have been compiled with the greatest care by the author. However, neither the author nor the publisher can assume liability, guarantee or warranty for the correctness, completeness and topicality. The author and the publisher hereby expressly declare that at the time the links were created, no illegal content was discernible on the linked pages. The author and the publisher have no influence whatsoever on the current and future design, content or authorship of the linked pages. Therefore, they hereby expressly distance themselves from all content that was changed after the link was set.

**Image credits:** Book cover Image by rawpixel ("foto tropische blätter_4191330") on freepik.com; author portrait and images of the flat, furniture and clothing, own image.

*Holistay - How I travel at home
to always be on holiday*

# Content

# Foreword

I don't have to go far to travel. I don't even have to pack my suitcase to experience an adventure. Often it is enough to step outside the door and I am immersed in an exciting experience. Life itself is a source of pure joy, I am firmly convinced of that! Every day there is something new to discover. You just have to look more closely.

Travelling is not only about experiences that we proudly report and fondly remember later, but above all about having time for yourself. Time to switch off, relax and finally have a good night's sleep. Holidays are about doing things we hardly find time for otherwise: Meeting friends, doing sports, being creative or simply putting our feet up. So holidays are often a contrast to the otherwise so routine, sometimes hectic and stressful everyday life. People who like to travel are often interested in foreign cultures, languages and traditions. The encounter with the foreign can enrich, sensitise and expand knowledge. Fortunately, this experience does not depend on the distance of a journey. Further does not equal better.

All the longings, desires and dreams that we seek to realise on our journeys can be fulfilled in any form of being on the road. A (physical) journey is ultimately always a journey to oneself. Unforgettable encounters, great adventures, deep relaxation, the feeling of freedom, the "paradise on earth" can be goals of a long-distance journey, but they can also be found where you are, at home.

So if we do it right, we don't have to fill our holiday coffers, wait for our annual leave, pack our bags, get on the plane and leave the country. Our holiday starts now - Holistay!

The term "Holistay" is a creative English word combination of "Holiday" and "Stay" and means something like "to holiday at home" or "travelling at home". A similar term is "staycation", which is a combination of "stay" and "holiday". Both terms were probably coined during the economic crisis in the USA to encourage people to spend their next holiday at home.

Let's not misunderstand each other: I love to travel! Especially my homelands, which I explore on foot, by bike, bus and train, and above all at a pleasantly slow pace. Of course, I have also been to foreign countries and to the other side of the globe. I also travel all over Germany for work. But long journeys are exhausting and often everything happens much too fast. There is a folk belief of the ancient Native Americans that at the speed we travel today, the soul often doesn't keep up. That's how I feel sometimes too! Over the years I have even developed a kind of fear of flying, which I would rather call flight antipathy.

Many European cities and popular holiday destinations are massively overcrowded anyway. Cities like Venice, Barcelona, Lisbon, Prague, Berlin, Amsterdam, Vienna, New York and

Athens are bursting at the seams. But Croatia, Iceland, Majorca, Hungary, Denmark and Singapore are also virtually flooded with tourists. The country and its people suffer. The traveller doesn't have much fun either, I think. But I don't want to debate too much about overtourism or trace ecological footprints now, I'd rather focus on my own footprints on the ground and take it all at a pleasantly slow pace.

---

**A brief history of travel**

Since time immemorial, man has been on the move. He is constantly on the move, so to speak, even if the motives have changed greatly over time.

Originally, humans explored new habitats for reasons of necessity - the search for food, water, safety - but also out of curiosity about what lay beyond the horizon. About 300,000 years ago, Homo sapiens left Africa in search of new resources, as archaeological finds in Morocco show. It was not until about 10,000 years ago that humans settled down, practised agriculture and animal husbandry and built villages and cities. At the same time, planned travel for economic and religious reasons also began: Pilgrimages, slave trade and messenger services caused people to leave their homes and travel. Thus, travelling became an important part of the history of human development.

Middle Ages

A journey in the Middle Ages (6th-15th centuries) was primarily religious or commercially motivated. Pilgrims (monks) or merchants usually set out on foot or horseback, but there were neither roads nor bridges. Even maps could not be relied upon. The Italian merchant Marco Polo (13th century) is said to have travelled China overland for the first time via the famous Silk Road. Such a journey was of course very arduous and not infrequently life-threatening. The travellers were attacked by wild animals, but also by robbers, and sometimes it took half a lifetime.

The conquest of the seas

In the late Middle Ages (15th century), the seas and with them new continents such as Asia, Africa and America were finally opened up by ship. Today, however, it is assumed that seafaring is much older. The first boats for fishing were built as early as the Stone Age. With the help of these boats, even the coasts of East Asia are said to have been reached in 40,000 BC. This would at least explain how people reached South America via Alaska and the continent. Officially, the first ships were built around 7,000 BC in Greece and the Canary Islands. Detailed depictions of ships on papyrus scrolls of the ancient Egyptians (5,000 BC) and on pottery shards in South Korea bear witness to this.

Migration and crusades

Time and again there were so-called migratory movements, i.e. groups of people who set out to settle new lands (often by fighting, war and conquest). A great migration of peoples took place between the 4th and 6th centuries. During this time, various Germanic tribes advanced south, west and east, especially from the north. At the same time, the Slavs spread further and further west, which probably led to the gradual disintegration of the Roman Empire that ruled at the time.

The Christian-motivated crusades took place mainly in the 11th and 13th centuries. So-called crusaders went east in the name of Christianity to spread and defend their faith and to fight against increasing Islamisation. The Crusades have gone down in history as bloody and cost many lives.

The Grand Tour of the Nobility

In the 18th and 19th centuries, it was mainly aristocrats who went on journeys. This form of educational and pleasure travel was called a "Grand Tour". The aristocratic elite became acquainted with foreign languages and arts, made valuable contacts and at the same time enjoyed the pleasure and entertainment programme in the flourishing cities. The most important centres were Italy, England and France. But the Alps, the Baltic Sea and the North Sea were also popular destinations. This century contributed to the fact that the longing for "unspoiltness", "originality" and "freedom" was increasingly projected onto distant destinations.

Written fixation of travel

The printing press in particular (around 1440 AD) made it possible to make travel literature and thus access to foreign worlds accessible to a broad public through writing. Matthäus Merian is considered a pioneer of travel literature (17th century). Karl Baedeker founded the first German publishing house for travel guides. For the first time, travellers could now prepare for their upcoming trip with tips and information. Such a travel guide quickly became a guide suitable for the masses. Hotels were categorised, places were classified as "important", sights were named and tourist flows were systematically directed - until today.

Industrialisation and the emergence of the package holiday

A little later, the first travel agencies were founded in England under the name Thomas Cook. Organised travel groups of the upper middle classes explored the world for the first time (19th century) and tried to escape the pressure to perform at the time. Egypt in particular was popular as a holiday destination.

With industrialisation, travel finally became suitable for the masses. After the First World War, holidays were made legally possible for the working classes for the first time. Sea travel became more and more popular and technical development and the expansion of rail and road transport, and since the 1970s also air transport, made holiday travel to faraway countries possible.

After the Second World War, more and more people could afford a holiday trip. Suddenly, mail-order companies like Neckermann and Quelle as well as the ADAC also got involved in the tourism industry and offered holiday trips at affordable prices. Since the 1960s, the tourism industry has been booming in modern industrialised countries and it is hard to imagine the calendar without (package) holidays. Popular destinations were above all Majorca, South Tyrol, Southern France and the Spanish mainland.

Alternative travel

But not everyone is satisfied with the "massification of travel", the complete organisation and standardisation of holidays. A counter-movement with a non-binding character is developing. This alternative form of travel takes place, for example, via Interrail, by hitchhiking or by caravan. The so-called hippie trail emerges and leads from Europe to South Asia - often via country roads and with backpacks. Popular destinations included Ibiza, Formentera, Morocco, Afghanistan, Nepal and India. Musicians like Jimi Hendrix, the Rolling Stones and the Beatles also contributed to the popularity of these places as enthusiasts and lovers.

It was at a rickety kitchen table in a hostel somewhere in Singapore that the first Lonely Planet, entitled "Across Asia on the Cheap", was finally written by Tony and Maureen Wheeler, two young backpackers from England. The Lonely Planet differs from other travel literature in that it promises individual and independent travel tips away from the tourist crowds and typical sights.

But this form of travel has also changed. Digitalisation is not only giving travel agencies a hard time, but will probably soon replace the last printed travel guide under the arm with smartphone apps.

# Holistay instead of far away

Holistay in this context means that the journey begins right on your doorstep. Not infrequently, it is a journey to oneself. But no, this is not about a spiritual search for the true self or a critical examination of mass tourism and the praise of local travel.[1] It is not my intention to discourage globetrotters from their adventures, to criticise them or to convince them otherwise. Nor is this book a local travel guide extolling the virtues of domestic travel. Nor is it a guidebook à la "Balkonien - wie man seinen Balkon wunderbar nutzen".

My idea stems from my enthusiasm for what, on closer inspection, takes place before our eyes - no matter where and how we live. I also firmly believe that our homes and the way we spend our free time are essential for relaxing and recharging our batteries. Our free time is made for strengthening social relationships, learning new craft skills, playing a musical instrument or learning a foreign language, developing creatively and keeping our bodies fit. In our free time, we can finally explore our surroundings, visit neighbouring towns, celebrate city festivals, go for long walks and

---

[1] Those who are nevertheless interested in the topic should read the following critical studies on tourism, for example by the writer and editor Hans Magnus Enzensberger and the futurologist, political and economic consultant Horst W. Opaschowski. Also worth mentioning are Norbert Suchanek's overview study "Die dunklen Seiten des globalisierten Tourismus" (The dark sides of globalised tourism") from the APUZ series 47 from 2001 and the monograph "Der ganz normale Reisewahn. Wie Tourismus abgrast den Planeten" by Stephan Bernau from 2015. Further information on the topic is available on the websites www.fairunterwegs.org and www.tourismuswatch.com.

hikes - in short, we can go travelling. From my point of view, there is little time for long-distance travel.[2]

Shouldn't we focus our search for fun, adventure, relaxation, meaning in life, friendship and joy much more on our surroundings, our home and fellow human beings, our partner, good friends, neighbours and nice colleagues? Do we really have to fly to the other end of the world to be happy, relaxed and free? Certainly not. So what is it really about?

**Tourism today and CO2 emissions**

Travelling today has changed yet again. Nothing is unusual any more. A holiday on the Balearic Islands or Lake Garda is no longer enough. Today, it can be a trip around the world: a shopping weekend in New York, a bachelor party in Las Vegas, a wellness weekend in Dubai or a skiing holiday in South Africa - nothing is impossible - and that is somehow disconcerting. The holiday trip lasting several weeks has become an integral part of our modern lives.

---

[2] In the travelogues of proud globetrotters you often hear that they have left everything behind: career, car, house, furniture. They trade "freedom for security" and "adventure for routine". The special thing about Holistay, however, is that you don't necessarily have to give up your "secure job", sell all your possessions and leave your life behind to finally be "free" and experience the "adventure of a lifetime". One is encouraged to "break out of the grip of everyday life", "finally feel life", "make friends", "get to know foreign cultures" and above all "get to know oneself better". But wait, I think. This sounds suspiciously like an elaborate sales strategy and a potentially dangerous game with our dreams! Of course it is important to take time out from life from time to time, especially when it seems to be going over your head or in the wrong direction. Escaping from everyday life can be healing in many ways. But this is often much easier than a long-distance trip or a trip around the world, where you might have to start all over again, which is often undertaken out of frustration and not infrequently amounts to an escape.

We no longer consider travel a luxury or something out of the ordinary, nor do we want to give up this privilege. We have become accustomed to the huge choice and variety, so that we often no longer think about possible consequences or even absurdities.

To give a small overview:

Our modern lifestyle has led to an alarming increase in $CO_2$ emissions worldwide. Each of us contributes our share, whether it is using electronic devices such as laptops, heating our homes in winter or taking a shower every day. It may come as a surprise that one hour of laptop use causes a comparatively low 12 g of $CO_2$, while a seemingly harmless hot shower already releases 3 kg of $CO_2$. Heating in the winter months can even emit up to 9.5 kg of $CO_2$ per day, which underlines the importance of energy efficiency and sustainable heating measures.

The figures from myclimate.org are alarming and show that the average $CO_2$ consumption of a person in the EU is between 9,000 and 11,000 kg per year. This corresponds to four times the annual value of about 2,600 kg $CO_2$ per person, which is calculated as "tolerable". Such high $CO_2$ emissions have far-reaching consequences for our environment and climate, such as rising global temperatures, acidification of the oceans, melting of the polar ice caps and loss of biodiversity.

One way from A to B:

From Hamburg to Munich = 310 kg $CO_2$ per flight/ per person

From Berlin to Hurghada (Egypt) = 1,725 kg $CO_2$ per flight/ per person

From Stuttgart to Dubai = 2,614 kg $CO_2$ per flight/ per person

A 10-day trip on a cruise ship = 2,900 kg $CO_2$ per person

From Frankfurt to New York = 3,100 kg CO2 per flight/ per person

From Nuremberg to Japan = 6,046 kg CO2 per flight/ per person

From Düsseldorf to Hawaii = 8,418 kg CO2 per flight/ per person

So, if you fly once from Germany to Dubai, you already reach the recommended annual per capita average. To put this into perspective, someone who drives a medium-sized car an average of 12,000 km a year only consumes about 2,000 kg of CO2 per year. It is interesting to note that even if someone were to eat beef steaks for a whole year - to illustrate the absurdity - the CO2 emissions per person would only be about 1,800 kg.

# Where does the desire to travel all the time come from?

No matter how far we travel, our own four walls are still the most beautiful place of retreat. Here we can find peace, relax and find ourselves. Of course, this requires that we feel completely comfortable and secure in our home.

That is why it is important to ask ourselves: How do I actually live? Do I feel comfortable? Do I like my home? Because the more we feel disturbed or uncomfortable within our own four walls, the louder the call for distance and change. So it is worthwhile to observe one's surroundings closely, listen to one's inner self and think about what small changes we can make in the here and now to make every evening at work truly relaxing.

An example of this is my good friend who works in industry and has a good income. She has afforded herself a spacious, bright 2-room flat with a balcony in a central location near her parents' house. She has furnished the flat with great attention to detail; the generous corner couch and the impressively large flat-screen TV in the living room are particularly striking.

She has also acquired a considerable wine collection, which she uses almost daily to ring in the end of the day with friends or during spontaneous visits from her parents. The premium gym, of which she is of course a member, is just around the corner and the city centre is only a ten-minute walk away. At first glance, everything seems perfect. But despite all these conveniences, she hardly has any time for herself. The daily commute to her workplace alone, which she can only reach by car, takes at least two hours. Overtime is not uncommon in her job. In addition, she has decided to continue her education on the side to improve her career opportunities. This means additional stress after work and at weekends.

When I visit, I am also always struck by the many photos taken in different places around the world: Northern Lights in Scandinavia, the breathtaking Napali Coast in Hawaii, the majestic Machu Picchu in Peru, the fascinating Angkor Wat in Cambodia and much more. She loves to travel and has taken more and more opportunities to do so in recent years. Every holiday day is already planned for the next unknown destination. She hardly spends any time in her beautifully furnished flat.

One evening I realised why this is so: when it gets quiet in the flat, sounds from the neighbouring flats suddenly reach her. Not only can she follow the news on TV, but she can also hear the old pensioner talking to himself during the programme. And involuntarily, she also hears the neighbours' marital quarrel every evening, as I myself have to witness. All this triggers unease in me. I feel less and less at ease. Now I also understand why she prefers to go to her parents to study rather than stay in her own flat.

When I ask her about it, she is a little surprised. She has never consciously noticed or thought about the noises from the neighbouring flats. Her urge to just be away and explore the wide world is simply there for her. Where this constant wanderlust comes from, she can't explain exactly. I guess it's a kind of escape from everyday life. Instead of moving or reducing her working hours, she seems to compensate for the discomfort in her own four walls (and perhaps also the additional pressure in her career) by travelling.

Of course, not every desire to travel is due to discomfort, stress or dissatisfaction in everyday life. We also travel for pure pleasure, curiosity, the joy of discovery and the desire for the unknown. The fascination of the unfamiliar has always attracted us. We appreciate the feeling of freedom, light-heartedness and being unbound. Sometimes we long for variety, inspiration and not infrequently we look for extraordinary experiences or even paradise on earth.

However, it is clear that we do not necessarily always find these things on the "outside", but that we often already carry them within ourselves. It might be worthwhile to listen more closely to ourselves and ask ourselves what actually drives us.

# Brief scientific background

For more than 13 years I have been working on the topic of tourism from a cultural studies perspective. In my master's thesis at the University of Heidelberg, I focused on the topic of "religious tourism and marketing". I analysed travel guides and their portrayal of religions. I not only examined how this representation has changed over time and with each new edition, but also which specific patterns of description can be found in the travel guides. Religions have always been popular as tourist "markers" in other countries. They serve as an attraction in a foreign culture, be it in the form of a festival or a holy site that can be visited. They offer opportunities for encounter, but are also marketed accordingly and often adapted for tourism. One could also extend the concept of religion to the more general concept of culture and ask how touristified or "Disneyfied" one's own journey already is and what about it is still authentic at all.

For me, travel is always a tightrope walk between actual encounters, cultural exchange and consumption. In doing so, I ask myself whether it is at all possible to organise travel in such a way that both the travellers and the local people benefit from it. I have friends who travel all over the world. They save large sums of money, take sabbaticals, rent out their flat and embark on a big trip around the world. Some of them run travel blogs or even have their own YouTube channel where they share their experiences with the whole world. Although many of them visibly strive to be close to the people on the ground, most travellers end up just staying in their own bubble. This can have several reasons. The focus is often on their own needs and experiences. Every traveller brings certain expectations with them, which not infrequently lead to stereotypes, unconscious prejudices and misunderstandings (often due to language barriers or social differences) and often one finds oneself in a tourist bubble created by the tourism industry with deliberately little contact with the local population. But the question is, at what price?

Not only does world travel consume enormous amounts of resources such as energy, water and food, mass tourism can also lead to commercialisation and the loss of authentic local culture. Traditions, customs and ways of life can be displaced or changed by the adaptation to tourist needs and the pressure of mass tourism. Overcrowding, pollution and damage to natural and cultural sites are often the result, but so are social inequalities, as only a few benefit from tourism while the local population suffers from low wages and precarious working conditions. Many developing countries rely heavily on the tourism sector as their main source of income. This dependence can lead to an unhealthy imbalance where local economies and infrastructure are neglected and communities become vulnerable to economic shocks and crises.

**Travel motives today**

- Relaxation from the stresses of everyday life or work

- Curiosity and the desire for variety

- Enjoying a better climate and good weather

- Desire for a good time and the feeling of happiness and freedom

- Special interest in culture, language and people

- The desire to discover unknown places

- Freedom from obligations and the daily grind

- Time for oneself to pause and become aware of oneself

- Exploring boundaries and broadening horizons

- Gathering new impressions and inspiration

- Reflecting back and appreciating what you already have

# Places that you must have seen

Some people keep so-called "bucket lists". These self-imposed life plans are a compilation of places they want to visit or things they want to experience before they pass away. Some of my acquaintances have a map of the world hanging in their kitchen, on which they put more and more pins to mark the places they have already visited. The world is big. They still have a lot to do. And just imagine if all the inhabitants of this earth came up with this idea! If you look at some vlogs (video contributions on YouTube), you might think that the idea of the "adventure society" is already taking on extreme proportions here.

Nevertheless, I would like to emphasise here that this perhaps explains why I personally don't like to get on a plane. If everyone feels like they do, I don't want to be part of it! I don't want to. I'm happy to do without and prefer to stay here!

I don't want to make any universal judgements about the actual motivations for (long-distance) travel. Rather, I want to share my enthusiasm for what we can already find on our doorstep. Because personally, I don't wait for my annual holiday, but simply bring the holiday feeling home. I'll show you how to do that on the following pages. Do you already have wanderlust or rather homesickness? Then join me on the next few pages. I'll be happy to take you on my journey home.

But before you really get started, you should follow these rules to make your trip an unforgettable dream holiday. Are you ready? Here are my personal tips:

# Holistay Rules

-   Switch off all electrical devices such as mobile phones, computers, televisions, e-books and microwaves as often as possible.

-   Avoid answering the phone while you are on holiday. If someone from work finds out that you are home, you may have to be on call.

-   Resolve to take off your watch and turn off your alarm clock. It's interesting to find out what makes your body clock tick.

-   Put the camera away, don't use social media and don't answer emails.

-   Put your to-do lists aside and postpone housework and repairs until another time.

- Inform relatives, acquaintances and friends that you are taking a "holiday" and taking time for yourself. Make it clear that you are not available.

- Leave the car, walk a lot or use your bike instead.

- Reduce your consumption of coffee, wine, beer, cola, chocolate, cakes, cigarettes and other stimulants that you may over-consume.

- Try to avoid busy shopping streets, supermarkets and crowded places. Stay away from roads and noisy traffic.

- Ignore news, advertising and negative headlines of any kind.

- Also avoid people who are in a bad mood, constantly nagging and grumbling for no reason - you are free now!

My journey: Four Walls, Four
Directions & Me

# Holiday feeling in everyday life

When I close my eyes and think of my last holiday, the image of Rügen, an enchanting Baltic Sea island off the coast of Western Pomerania, arises in my mind's eye. The small island enchants with countless bays, breathtaking chalk cliffs, picturesque thatched and spa villages, dense beech forests, wide sandy beaches and imposing cliffs.

A whole week ahead of me and packed only with a small 20-litre backpack, I set off. My modest luggage consists of two pairs of leggings, two training jackets (one of which doubles as a weatherproof sports jacket), a couple of tops, running shoes, sandals and a beenie to protect me from the cool Baltic wind. My journey begins in Bergen, the central town on the island. My plan is to change hotels every two days - a kind of island hopping, if you will.

My first hotel turns out to be a real stroke of luck: sauna, a rich buffet and evening entertainment in the middle of town. My room is clean, flooded with light and smells pleasantly of lavender. From the first moment, I can relax completely here. Of course, the TV stays off during my stay. I even refrained from taking something to read with me. This way I can concentrate fully on what is in front of me.

In the next few days, extensive cycling tours are on the agenda, during which I will cover many kilometres. Luckily, I can rent a mountain bike directly at the hotel. The route takes me along lakes, through Jasmund National Park, up to Cape Arkona and along the impressive chalk cliffs. On my bike tours I collect beautiful flints, which I later throw back into the sea. Spontaneously, I also decide to take a ride on the traditional railway, the "Rasender Roland" ("Roland the Paddler"). I take long walks along the Bodden beaches, visit the seaside resort of Prora, explore a submarine museum, walk barefoot along the beach early in the morning and enjoy live music in a cosy beach bar in the evening. In between, I always allow myself a little nap, drink tea and let my gaze wander enchanted over the wide sea. Once the weather has changed, I simply visit the nearby indoor swimming pool.

How quickly time flies! At the end of the week, I get reflective and think about how I can integrate the wonderful time I have had here into my everyday life. Because nothing spectacular actually happened. Nevertheless, I really like how I spent my days and I would like to feel this good every day (even in everyday life). I ask myself why I always have to wait for my holiday instead of creating such experiences in my everyday life as well. Is such a holiday only possible because it is a contrast to everyday life? Is it only special because it happens so rarely? What did I actually experience that was so extraordinary that I couldn't have done on my doorstep?

# My little holiday home

Forest, water, walks, restaurants, music, museums and meeting nice people - I actually find all that here too. What I lack, however, is time, space (the "right" facilities) and above all the serenity to let myself go for it like on holiday. But I am firmly convinced that this is also possible. I can bring the holiday home!

So, step by step, I have been working on my concept of integrating holidays into my everyday life: Due to my professional flexibility, I moved back to Heidelberg, the city where I studied and lived six years before. My current flat is a little smaller, but very centrally located - and for the first time I have a south-facing balcony. Heidelberg is known as a city for its high cost of living. In fact, it is one of the fourth most expensive cities in Germany, along with Munich, Hamburg and Frankfurt am Main. But Heidelberg also offers a lot of what you imagine a perfect holiday destination to be: the Odenwald, the Neckar, the old town, a diverse cultural offering, numerous opportunities to party, learn and further your education, good transport connections, shopping opportunities, student flair and beautiful nature right on the doorstep!

During my last move, I finally decided to stop cluttering my rooms with superfluous furniture, decorative items, closets full of clothes, memorabilia or collections. My goal is to engage with everything new every day without anything "getting in the way". Years ago, I said goodbye to all the material ballast like souvenirs, supplies, rarely used items, useless gifts and other superfluous things. Even the last move went effortlessly by train and taxi. It was almost flattering that the taxi driver thought I was a student with my two suitcases.

Now I'm aiming for a style of living similar to that of a hotel suite or a holiday finca. The two rooms in my new flat don't need any elaborate decoration. The rooms are naturally beautiful, with wooden floors and large windows that offer a view of the sky! In my room, there is only my cosy, simple wooden bed that I have comfortably furnished with soft fabrics in white, taupe and anthracite. The walls are white and reflect a lot of daylight. In the evening, I switch my daylight lamp to twilight and can read a little in my book before I get tired and fall asleep. Except for the lamp, all electronic devices are banned from the room. Just like on holiday, work has no place in the bedroom. It's a room for cuddling and relaxing.

In my second room, the living room, there is only my yoga mat. Here I have enough space to lie in the sun, meditate, dance, leaf through magazines, draw, read or listen to music. I call this room my little yoga studio because here I can completely switch off and move in all directions.

I have set up a personal coffee corner in my kitchen, which is also my creative workspace. I create an inspiring atmosphere at a simple bar table with comfortable stools. This place is a retreat for me where I can fully dedicate myself to my freelance work. Here I find everything I need to push ahead with my projects and give free rein to my creativity without any major distractions. And of course, I can't do without a cup of delicious coffee to accompany me through my productive hours and give me the energy I need.

What I particularly appreciate about my flat is the fact that it literally invites me to immediately set off for the next activity. Whether I want to relax in nature, stroll through the winding alleys of the old town, unwind by the water or browse in the vastness of a library - everything is right on my doorstep. Heidelberg offers me a wealth of opportunities that I like to use to make my life varied and exciting.

In this context, I have also changed the way I deal with books. I now always pass on copies I've read immediately instead of collecting them on the shelf. This way I can rid myself of things I no longer need and give other people pleasure at the same time. It is liberating to no longer carry around ballast and to make room for new experiences and memories.

I'm actually a big proponent of digitisation, of e-books and cloud computing. I hardly own any paper anymore. But since my internet provider let me down a bit and I became aware of my dependence on this electronic service, I try to have at least a few important books and documents at home and find a certain middle ground.

Now everything has its fixed place, nothing stands around and above all I save time on housework. I haven't needed a hoover, dishwasher or tumble dryer for a long time, neither shelves nor a television. And a living room couch would only get in the way.

The few things that enrich my everyday life, apart from the bed, table and laptop, include only a few accessories such as candles, flowers or pictures. The number of things I own since my big decluttering campaign over five years ago hasn't changed since then: 300 things! For me, this is the perfect amount to enjoy more free space, simplify organisation and realise the holiday feeling in everyday life. I gain time that I would otherwise have spent tidying, searching, caring, repairing, etc.

---

**Everything can, but nothing has to**

Why not take a holiday at home, where it is most beautiful? Staying at home can be really fun, especially when you explore the surroundings and see your own place of residence with new eyes. There is so much to discover and from the first minute you feel the deceleration of the holiday! You save yourself the stress of planning your trip, packing your suitcase, driving to the airport, parking, waiting and queuing. Interesting museums, green parks and cosy cafés are also available in my city and immediate surroundings. Finally you have time for friends, a visit to the zoo or a little boat trip on the river or lake. You can eat ice cream, browse through books, climb towers. How about a walk in the woods, a bike ride or a relaxing wellness evening with all the trimmings? You can go out for a delicious meal, to the cinema or straight to a concert. Yoga, cabaret, opera, ice skating. Swimming pool, stadium or beer garden. But above all, you have plenty of time to sleep in, to start the day relaxed, without appointments and time pressure. Countless possibilities, but no obligations - that should not only be the motto for the next holiday, but for every day at home!

# Your own flat - a fabulous place for holidays

Switching to holidays at home can be a real challenge at first, and it took me some time to get the hang of it too. Apart from the time aspect - because we all have little time for the big spring cleaning, smaller renovations or even moves - the spatial possibilities also play an important role. The decisive factor is, of course, where you live. I was lucky that after school and university I always lived in cities that were big enough and always had something touristy about them: whether Heidelberg, Landau or Nuremberg.

But in principle, every place has something interesting to offer. With a little imagination, every town and every village is suitable for a "holistay". If you are open to new things, curious about life and like to learn new things in everyday life, you don't have to go far away. The horizon - whether physical or mental - can also be constantly expanded in this country.

Practically speaking, however, we have the design of our home in our hands. We can change it according to our mood and thus create a little holiday feeling. How exactly do we do that? I like to think back to my last trip, to the beautiful hotel rooms. I always have bright, clean rooms in mind that are, above all, free of clutter. Everything that doesn't belong in the beautiful hotel suite has to "get out". Removing or rearranging furniture or replacing it with simple, timeless furniture would be conceivable. It doesn't have to cost much and you can simply research on the internet and get inspired under keywords like "hotel room", "hotel suite", "finca", "studio flat" or "minimalist living". Is there something that appeals? Where would one feel particularly comfortable and what gives rise to a holiday mood? What could your own room or flat look like to make you feel like you're on holiday? And how can you make it happen?

Let's take another look around our own room and consider the status quo. Your own four walls are probably still far from what you imagine as a holiday idyll - there is probably still too much furniture standing around, the cupboards are full of clothes, folders and objects and somehow the colours don't really match yet. Where do you start? I have a very simple solution: simply turn the tables. Don't think about what doesn't belong, but what can stay. In principle, there are only six areas that you should pay attention to in your furnishings:

1. A cosy bed with a comfortable mattress and beautiful bed linen to feel good. Here it is essential to ensure that the bed linen is single-coloured, always freshly washed and preferably made of compatible natural materials. There should not be too many pillows, blankets and preferably no soft toys on the bed. 2.

2. A storage facility for the clothes, be it a wardrobe, a simple clothes rail, a nice box or even a suitcase (depending on the space). Again, the more colourful the

clothes, the more cluttered the room. A wardrobe door or a curtain can provide visual calm.

3. A table is a must - but which is the right one? Whether it's a dining table with chairs, a standing table, a folding table or a side table - the back should decide (after all, we spend many hours here).

4. Perhaps a small additional shelf with doors to store household or office supplies, important files, books, the make-up bag as well as towels and bed linen that are needed daily, out of sight.

5. Of course, you need a kitchen (you can't always eat out), but in my opinion a kitchenette (kitchen unit) equipped with the essentials is enough: a few plates, bowls, glasses, cutlery, a kettle, an (external) induction plate, maybe a toaster and a small oven. With these, you can conjure up delicious dishes without spending a lot of time in the kitchen.

6. A washing machine is also a must, because you don't always want to run to the launderette. You can either put it in the laundry room or buy a compact toploader.

# Only the favourite clothes

The Holistay campaign is even easier when it comes to clothes. First, my wardrobe is subjected to a thorough inspection. I want to focus on the essentials and only keep the clothes that I really like and feel completely comfortable in. A large part of my wardrobe consists of basics that can be combined in many ways and offer me flexibility in putting together my outfits. I consciously choose clothes that I can wear often, because individual pieces that are only worn on certain occasions no longer have any place here.

My wardrobe contains a few plain T-shirts, leggings, knee-length dresses, underwear, a few blouses and three pairs of jeans. In addition, there are neutral jumpers, cardigans and blazers that give me a simple and timeless look in various combinations. When it comes to shoes, I focus on functionality and comfort and therefore own sports shoes, sneakers, sandals, ballerinas and ankle boots - a total of five pairs that I can fall back on in different situations (and weather conditions!). I am well prepared for the different seasons and own a winter jacket, an autumn coat, a rain jacket and a transitional jacket - four pieces that always keep me suitably dressed.

In addition to clothes, I also have some accessories that give my outfit the finishing touch but above all prepare me for the changing weather: Scarf, hats, gloves and an umbrella are important companions that I can't do without. All my clothes are in black, grey, brown, beige or blue, so I don't have to worry about possible combinations. This way, I can effortlessly put together different outfits while maintaining the minimalist and timeless style that has come to define me. In any case, I never ask myself "what should I wear?

When I'm out and about, I only have my 20-litre backpack with me, which contains the essentials: a pair of trousers, a dress, a burlap bag, scarves and always something to write with. In summer, it's much easier to be on the road because the light clothes don't take up so much space in the backpack. Moreover, it is quickly washed in the evening and dry again overnight. So I practically have half my home with me - that's all I need.

With this targeted selection of my favourite pieces and the focus on timeless basics, I feel not only well equipped for any occasion, but also freed from superfluous ballast. The Holistay action in my wardrobe takes away the "agony of choice". It helps me to always focus on the essentials and to always feel authentic and comfortable in my outfits.

My entire wardrobe now fits into my 80-litre suitcase (centre). I also have a shoulder bag (the only one!) in which I always have the most important things like a calendar, smartphone, laptop, umbrella and bicycle pump at hand. What you don't see here is my rental bike, which I subscribe to monthly. I cycle up to 10 kilometres a day and haven't needed a car for a long time.

# Digital or analogue?

When the bookshelf is about to collapse and the pile of books on the bedside table feels like it reaches under the ceiling, it's high time to read, isn't it?! No, seriously! We should only have the books with us that we really want to read, that make us feel good, that teach us something new, that take us further, that show us a new world with new ideas, that inspire and fulfil us. Whether or not to keep books after reading them should not be defined too strictly. Books are something like friends. They speak to us, encourage, comfort and help us, and in the best case more than once!

I have gotten into the habit of excerpting (before passing on) good books that I know I won't have to read again. Yes, it takes work and time, but in doing so I consciously deal with them again and put down on paper what is essential for me. Only then can I give them away without a guilty conscience. If I don't find time for a summary, I will probably never find the time to read the whole book again, will I? Because of my concerns about the aforementioned dependence on the internet, I make sure to have at least some printed copies and reference books at home. To be honest, I also prefer to read on paper before going to bed at night rather than on a screen.

# Naturally at home and naturally relaxing

Nature has always had a special, calming and healing effect on us humans. So why not rethink the decoration of your own four walls in the course of the Holistay action? As I said, only clean, fresh-smelling and minimalist living spaces come to mind when I think of holidays. Everything is uncluttered, tidy, clean and cosy.

A contradiction? Because nature itself is anything but tidy. It is rather chaotic. Outside, nothing is neatly arranged or dusted off. Yet the overall picture radiates harmony and perfection. The elements are always in balance: earth, water, sky (air) and sun (fire). The colours of nature are often strong, but never obtrusive. They have a calming effect, but never boring. When we walk through the forest, stroll by the lake, swim in the sea, trudge through the snow or climb, we feel the effect of nature. It appeals to all our senses. It is colourful and homogeneous at the same time and it always has a calming effect on us. So let us be inspired by nature as a source and make it a part of our home.

Nature offers beautiful materials that we can use directly: fresh flowers and houseplants, that's obvious. Everyone knows how beautiful flowers look on the windowsill, on the dining table or on the balcony. Hanging ivy, herb pots and dried flowers in pretty containers are also real eye-catchers. How about wood, pebbles, earth, sand, ceramics, grasses, bamboo, glass or cotton fabrics? You can even go one step further and consider eating your morning cereal out of a bamboo or coconut bowl, replacing plastic cans with glass jars or replacing the electric light with candlelight every now and then. Maybe you'll pick up a guitar again instead of streaming music from the internet, or knit yourself a winter hat instead of buying it in a sports shop. On the next hike, for example, you can look for beautiful stones or even shells that can be wonderfully used as decorative elements in your everyday finca. However, it is important to note that these items do not constitute an unintentional dwelling place for small animals that one unknowingly brings home. Furthermore, one should be aware that not all materials can simply be taken from the forest and placed at home. It is advisable to obtain information in advance whether collecting such materials is allowed in the area.

# Grounded and holistically refreshed

Our body, especially the feet, the eyes, even the gastrointestinal tract and of course the back need rest. Our feet need contact with the ground again, preferably in flat shoes. Our eyes need a break from the screen, our digestive system a break from coffee, sugar and acid. And above all, our backs need a break from sitting.

I too spend far too much time sitting, especially at work. In the meantime, I try to do without chairs as often as possible. Standing desks are a good evolution of our workplaces. More and more companies are upgrading and offering height-adjustable desks to their employees. Even if the purchase is not yet accepted by all companies. The trend towards standing is going in the right direction.

But how do I implement this in my private life? At home I do something for my back. It is moved, stretched, rolled and stretched - and I sit as little as possible. My standing table and yoga mat make sure of that. By the way, I have banned the sofa from my home because it tempted me too much after work. Instead, I now sit cross-legged on the floor more often, go for walks, jogs or maybe go to bed earlier (sleep plays an important role in Holistay, but more on that later). But if I feel like a cosy sofa, that's no problem of course! In the meantime, I know some very cosy places in my city, such as my favourite café, the reading room of the university library or the comfortable wing chair in the public library - most of the time they are still free. There really is no shortage of cosy places to sit here! And my guests? Most of us are happy about it and even grateful that we are on the move and not sinking into conversation on the sofa.

---

**Motion is everything**

In the course of a day, we sit for an average of 7.5 to 11 hours - at the breakfast table, in the car or on the train on the way to work, at our desk, at the dining table during our lunch break and on the sofa in the evening. It is alarming how much time we spend sitting. Even when we are actively doing sport: When cycling or in the gym, we adopt a sedentary posture again! In doing so, our muscles atrophy, our tendons shorten and our internal organs do not get enough blood supply. The entire musculoskeletal system is understrained every day. However, it is not only the sitting itself that harms our backs and causes so much pain. It is the lack of movement that is the real problem. Movement is the only way to effectively counteract back pain and the associated complaints and illnesses. It is important to move as often as possible, even during office work.

---

For me, the question of a TV doesn't arise because I said goodbye to the thing a long time ago. I wonder anyway when one finds time for it. It has always been a real time eater. Either you can't switch off or you zap through the programme for hours looking for something "worth watching".

If you want to decelerate your everyday life, really have time and consciously experience it, switch off the box. Of course, this also applies to computers (internet) and mobile phones, the "seducers" of our time! But as I said at the beginning about the Holistay rules: if we want to feel like we are on holiday, we should ignore them as often as possible, unless it is absolutely necessary.

For me, an evening without media is always like a journey to new ideas at a leisurely pace. This is wonderful in times of timelessness! The longer we spend in this media-free zone, the more relaxed we become. We immediately feel a deceleration, but also improved concentration and attention. We are more efficient, more relaxed and more creative. And our interpersonal relationships also improve - but only if our counterparts can also put their smartphones aside for a while.

# Sunny spots everywhere you look

Regardless of the current living situation, whether with my own balcony or a beautiful patio with an inviting bench, I always find a spot in the sun. I have made it a habit to use every free minute of the day to go outside and "soak up the light". Even when the sun is hiding behind clouds, I look for my little time outdoors, because even sparse daylight can work wonders. Even in the cold season, short trips outdoors do you good.

The importance of sunlight for our health is undisputed. Above all, vitamin D, which is actually a hormone, plays a decisive role and contributes significantly to our general well-being. Surprisingly, we take in 80 to 90 percent of our vitamin D needs through the skin, only 10 percent through food. This valuable substance is commonly known to strengthen the immune system, promote bone and dental health and support efficient fat metabolism. Even on cloudy days, our skin can absorb the vitamin.

There are other benefits to spending a few minutes in the sun each day. Just 10 minutes in daylight can have amazing effects on our sense of happiness. From mid-May, when the sun is higher in the sky and the temperatures are pleasant, you feel a tingling sensation on your skin. Sunlight stimulates the production of endorphins (happy hormones) that lift our mood and make us feel positive.

Our eyesight can even improve somewhat if we consciously turn towards the sun for a few minutes (but do not look directly into it, but keep our eyes closed).

And in winter? What do we do when the sun hides for days on end? There are solutions for that too: An infrared lamp can help. It generates pleasant warmth directly under the skin by emitting infrared rays. With such a lamp, we can enjoy this soothing warmth even when it is cold outside. Infrared light is mainly used in the medical and therapeutic field because of its positive effect on well-being. This type of light contains part of the sunlight spectrum, especially the beneficial red light, but does not emit any UV radiation. It is therefore particularly suitable for people who get little sunlight during the day. People with skin problems in the face, sinus problems or polyps can also benefit from infrared application. In addition, the pleasant deep warmth of infrared light is suitable for treating shoulder pain, local inflammation or sore muscles.

But you don't have to be "sick" to benefit from the advantages of infrared light. Even healthy people can use it. In winter, it is often the case that you leave the house in the dark in the morning and only return home from work after dark. - And this for a whole four months, from November to February. In such cases, the targeted use of infrared light can help compensate for the lack of natural sunlight and promote general well-being.

# To the balcony ares

Well, my balcony is not Ibiza or Mallorca and can never replace the Balearics. But the sun here is the same as on the holiday islands. When I relax on my balcony and close my eyes, it doesn't really matter where I am geographically. It's like being on holiday, only without a reserved mooring and without disturbing noise. I can decorate my balcony nicely, put up a few plants, add a string of lights, put up a parasol and provide cool drinks. From here I also have a wonderful view of the starry sky in the evening and I can also really enjoy thunderstorms from here.

There is a large tree in front of my balcony that is home to many songbirds, especially the blackbird. I used to pay little attention to the birds' songs, but now I am beginning to consciously notice the melodies and even pick out and recognise patterns. In early summer, the bird begins its concert at four in the morning and sings for almost three hours. And in the evening, the next bird enters the stage and gives its best. This solo performance also pleases the 40 or so cawing ravens that gather on the surrounding rooftops every evening - a truly amusing spectacle.

And we spend hundreds of euros on concert, theatre or opera tickets. Yet the most beautiful performance takes place every evening right outside our window.

**I'll just stay here**

Almost 60% of the French prefer to stay at home rather than travel. The same is true for 56% of Spaniards. Unsurprisingly, just over half of Italians value staying in their own country, as do half of Americans. One in three Austrians, Germans and Brazilians prefer to spend their holidays within their own four walls. Only 16% of Swiss and Belgians stay at home relatively rarely. They go travelling most often.

---

Another way to get in the mood for a holiday and get a feeling of freedom is to sleep in a sleeping bag on the balcony. Out of curiosity, I tried it a few times and was immediately impressed. Of course, I checked the weather forecast beforehand (you don't want to be surprised by rain) and then snuggled up in my blanket. It can get quite chilly at night. That's why I collected all kinds of blankets and wrapped myself up in them! Sleeping outside is a wonderfully liberating feeling. You are so close to the stars. The air is clear and fresh and you can see far into the distance. You become very humble out here. The next morning you feel like a new person.

---

**The story of the holiday on "Balcony"**

We love our balcony! It lends our living space a special charm and is especially coveted when it faces south. But what many take for granted today was a privilege in the 18th century that only aristocrats and intellectuals could afford. A city flat with a balcony was a sign of prosperity. These balconies served above all to present themselves to neighbours and society. In a sense, they were the private stage for self-expression.

Balconies were also increasingly built in the countryside, but for a completely different purpose. In winter, they served to cool food outdoors, as a kind of refrigerator substitute. In summer, herbs, fruit and vegetables were grown or dried here.

With industrialisation and housing construction, the balcony also made its way into the working class. It offered the opportunity to relax quickly after work. The balcony offered sunlight, fresh air and a small outdoor space.

In the 1930s, the term "Balkonien" emerged and even found its way into the Duden dictionary. When people started taking holidays at the Baltic Sea, in Italy or in the Alps, many longed for holidays at home. On the balcony you could grow your own vegetables, party with the neighbours and lie lazily in the sun. The balcony became the perfect place for a quick holiday in between - Balkonia.

# Four directions - where to go?

Of course, at Holistay we don't just sit on the balcony. Excursion destinations abound and they start right on the doorstep! You can set off in all four directions and always discover something new. It never gets boring, because if you are attentive, you will always come across unknown paths, undiscovered trails and turn-offs, even if you think you already know them all. There is always something to discover.

For example, when I walk west from the city centre, I leave the Heidelberg Forest behind. Passing the Bahnstadt, allotment gardens and sports fields, I reach Eppelheim. From there, my path leads me directly to a wide field being cultivated by hard-working farmers. A whiff of field scent is in the air, horses stand peacefully in their paddocks along the way. The route continues via Plankstadt to Schwetzingen. This charming destination offers the opportunity to stroll through the magnificent palace gardens or to stop for a drink in a cosy café.

If I walk further north on another day, I can walk directly along the Neckar. This path is particularly popular with joggers and cyclists, but as a pedestrian I still find peace and quiet and can enjoy nature. I pass the zoo, the Rhine-Neckar Olympic base, vegetable and strawberry fields and an organic farm with a relaxed cat sunning itself in the courtyard. I walk past restaurants, old half-timbered houses and always have the striking Dossenheim quarry and the Odenwald forest at my back. After about 11 kilometres of walking, I reach my destination: the beautiful medieval old town of Ladenburg. This town was founded by the Romans as early as 74 AD and was called "Lopodunum". Today it is one of the oldest towns in Germany.

If, on the other hand, I walk from the city centre in the opposite direction, i.e. east along the Neckar, I pass Heidelberg Castle, beautiful bridges and locks with impressive views of the densely overgrown Odenwald. I walk through the Neckartal-Odenwald Nature Park, which is one of the most beautiful hiking trails in Germany. However, you should not underestimate the road traffic here. An alternative is the Neckarsteig, a hiking trail directly through the forest. The landscape is overwhelming: passing the "Russenfels" ("Russian rock") quarry, an old monastery, green orchard meadows and campsites, I finally reach the last two districts of Heidelberg, which are connected by a bridge. Here I can stock up on provisions in a corner shop before continuing. Following the Neckar, I reach Neckargemünd after about 11 kilometres. The densely overgrown rocky hill right by the Friedensbrücke bridge in particular puts me in a holiday mood. Here you can camp directly on the Neckar, continue by boat or spontaneously rent a canoe. There are three other small towns in the Neckar valley, which together make up the "Romantic Four". Neckarsteinach, Hirschhorn and Eberbach are also wonderful places for a relaxing break, which can be reached by bus, train, bicycle or on foot. Anyone who is out and about here will forget about any long-distance destination.

The Odenwald is an area with many opportunities for exploration and discovery. It doesn't always have to be the road or the river, although that is of course convenient and safe. But the forest itself is a real highlight and is right on your doorstep. Anyone who has ever been to Heidelberg knows that the castle towers over the old town on a hill. Behind the ruins, the forest begins. Various hiking trails and even a traditional mountain railway lead up to the Königsstuhl. On the other side of the Königsstuhl is the Heiligenberg, which is easily reached via the famous Philosopher's Path. Up here are the Heidenloch, an impressive 55-metre-deep historical well, the famous Thingstätte, an open-air stage in the style of ancient Greek theatres, and the ruins of the Michaelskloster monastery dating from 1070. From here, the Odenwald, a varied landscape mosaic of mountains, meadows and mixed forests, stretches all the way to Darmstadt.

The south path leads me directly into the forest - a poem! After just a few steps, you are surrounded by nature. You enter a green oasis of peace. The ground is arched and covered with stones, branches, leaves and moss. Ferns and ivy adorn the edge of the path, branches are hung with buds, leaves and blossoms. Huge roots protrude from the ground. A spicy-fresh scent is in the air, and even on hot summer days it is pleasantly cool here. The background noise of the road traffic gives way to the gentle sounds of the forest. Sometimes you hear a woodpecker calling or spot a nimble squirrel. Butterflies flutter through the air and young tree branches dance in the wind. If you manage to walk through the forest early in the morning, you experience a completely different, almost surreal and long-forgotten world. The animals seem to be going crazy. Birds perform acrobatic flight manoeuvres, leaves whirl through the air and a forest concert resounds. And in fog, rain or at dusk, the forest radiates a magical-mythical atmosphere. You hear toads calling, see bats flying and, with a bit of luck, suddenly come face to face with a deer.

---

**Why the forest is good for us**

In our increasingly urbanised world, we are moving further and further away from natural habitats like the forest. At the same time, educational and therapeutic approaches are being developed to bring people closer to nature again. In fact, people are already talking about a "nature deficit" in our society. Scientists have rediscovered that the forest has significant and not to be underestimated positive effects on our body and psyche.

Even Aristotle emphasised the vital importance of the forest for our well-being and health. He recognised the influence of the forest on our ability to learn and concentrate. The so-called biophilia hypothesis states that humans always feel drawn to nature (to the living), can only develop in it and with all their senses, and only in this way become human beings. And this idea is not entirely absurd: after all, we are evolutionarily geared to interact with nature, to move within it, to adapt our habitat to it.

Current educational and therapeutic approaches aim to restore the connection between people and nature. Spending time in the forest not only promotes physical health, but also stress reduction, mood elevation and mental clarity. The forest offers us a retreat where we can relax, regenerate and rediscover our inner balance.

The forest is a true source of health. The air is clean and dust-free, and the trees release essential oils that cleanse our respiratory tract. It has been scientifically proven that spending time in the forest lowers blood pressure, reduces stress and can even help against depression. In the forest, adrenaline levels and the stress hormone cortisol decrease. It has even been observed that physical ailments subside when one spends time in nature. And who knows, maybe one day we will get the forest as a prescription. Japanese researchers have found out that the "mysterious power of trees" can even protect against diseases.

The forest has much more to offer. It holds a multitude of interesting remedies that we don't (no longer) know or have forgotten. Many of the edible roots and leaves contain bitter substances that are highly antioxidant and thus beneficial to health. However, we have trained our taste buds so much that we would hardly get them down. But these bitter substances can be very useful, such as the salicin contained in willow bark, which has a similar effect to aspirin. In addition, trees and plants give off so-called terpenes, natural organic compounds that enter the body when inhaled and activate the body's own defence cells. So our immune system benefits enormously from a walk in the forest.

In Japan, at any rate, "forest medicine" is now being pursued as an independent field of research. The Japanese are firmly convinced that forest air and regular forest walks have a positive influence on health and can even prolong life.

---

As soon as I enter the forest, I feel transported to another time, where nothing distracts me and nothing reminds me of modern life. The forest has a hypnotic effect, because I immediately sink into my thoughts as I take one step after the other. It's meditation at walking pace. On my walks I like to wear very flat shoes

(Barefoot shoes) to have maximum contact with the ground. That way I feel every stone and every branch. I deliberately walk very slowly. Sometimes, however, I walk a bit and breathe deeply in and out. It smells so good in the forest! The air acts like a natural filter. I also like the sound of dry leaves and find it pleasant to touch the bark of a tree or to collect leaves. I often puzzle over what kind of tree it is and try to refresh my knowledge of forest plants by looking at the leaves (forest education - when was that? Last time was probably primary school?). But even more exciting are the different species of birds. I can quickly identify a woodpecker, but what does the song of a titmouse, a sparrow or a pine grouse sound like? I've never seen a little owl and never heard a nightingale consciously singing.

I once attended a seminar on Olivier Messiaen (1908-1992) at the Musicological Institute in Heidelberg. The French composer, music teacher and organist is known for transcribing bird calls into notes. He was a close observer and possessed an absolute ear. Thus, he set out every morning shortly before four o'clock to listen to the various bird songs. He also collected bird songs on his travels around the world, which he incorporated into his famous works such as the Turangalila Symphony (which, however, takes some getting used to) and the orchestral piece Des Canyons aux Etoiles ("From the Canyons to the Mountains"). Wolfgang Amadeus Mozart, a great bird lover, also imitated all kinds of bird voices on the recorder. In his pieces, the voices of birds even appear as soloists.

Most birds sing to attract a mate or to mark their territory. The more intensely and loudly they sing, the more strongly they seem to pursue their intention. But not every bird is naturally a gifted performer: song behaviour depends strongly on environment, genetics and learning processes. You can find this out in your living environment. And you can pay attention to it.

No matter from where we start our little journey and in which direction we then move, there is always something exciting, worth knowing and thrilling to discover, right on our doorstep. All we have to do is set off.

# Bird's-eye view with Google Earth

In my childhood, I used to play on the game console from time to time. The Nintendo 64 in particular brought real innovation with the introduction of three-dimensional graphics. One of my favourite video games was, of course, Super Mario, which took me on rainy afternoons or school holidays into its fantastic world full of castles, clouds, volcanoes and underwater adventures. The different camera perspectives, which could be consciously controlled, made it possible to explore Mario's wonderful world. Especially the bird's eye view could be taken by controlling with the joystick to get an overview of the different themed worlds and, for example, to find out where the next "stars" (which had to be collected) were.

Nowadays, we have access to numerous online services that show our own city from a bird's eye view. This is not only interesting, but also very helpful in getting to know our surroundings better. We can now discover what is hidden behind the walls and explore places we would never have found otherwise. Green spaces, hidden parks, hiking trails or gardens can be easily found with the help of these services. We can also find shops, cafés or clubs that we might otherwise have overlooked.

The bird's eye view allows us to see the area as a whole and learn many things about our city that would not be visible to the naked eye.

In good balance:
Do something or better let it be

# Forgo the alarm clock and sleep in

If we were freed from the constraints of everyday life - without alarm clocks, noisy neighbours, whining children, appointments or telephones - when would we wake up naturally? When would we open our eyes, stretch out our arms, look out the window and decide it's time to get up?

Days off at weekends, holidays and, of course, on holiday offer us the unique opportunity to get back into this natural rhythm and finally sleep as long as we want without a guilty conscience. It has probably been a long time since our daily routine was no longer determined by strict schedules, social obligations or annoying tasks. Today, when we stay in bed longer, we often feel guilty. Some even think that we are oversleeping the day, not using our time wisely or even being lazy.

But what exactly are we missing out on when we decide to stay in bed a little longer, consciously rest and simply do nothing? What would be the alternative? Shopping, cooking, maybe cleaning the flat, going to the hairdresser, painting the garden fence, reading the newspaper, answering emails and surfing the internet? Those are nice prospects, aren't they?

If we are honest with ourselves, these are all just seemingly important tasks that never want to end and often trigger a chain reaction of further obligations. If instead we stay in bed a little longer, close our eyes once more and immerse ourselves in the world of dreams, we create the best foundation for starting the day refreshed, creative, with new energy and well-being.

## Offline

It's not only the alarm clock that pulls us out of our natural rhythm. It is even more difficult - as we all know - to put the smartphone aside for a while. The first thing many of us do when we wake up is look at our mobile phone. Not only does it serve as an alarm clock, but it is also at the dining table, on the desk and even at the workplace. We have the feeling that we must not miss anything. We constantly check whether new news has arrived or whether there is something new in the social media. Even during meetings with friends, conversations and appointments, the smartphone is always at hand and actively used.

In the 1990s, the mobile phone became popular for the ordinary consumer, which was gradually replaced by the smartphone (around 2007). Mobile devices offer many useful functions and great apps to make life easier and even save time. Reading street maps, visiting internet cafés, studying scoreboards or buying newspapers are no longer necessary. Today, we look at this device about 80 times a day - every 12 minutes. We use it to write, read, listen, watch, research, book, buy, play and entertain ourselves. We use it at every traffic light, in the queue, at the kitchen table and in bed. There is already the phenomenon of "mobile phone neck", which orthopaedists are increasingly warning about. Every year, about 300 people die in Germany because of distraction by mobile phones at the wheel (and the trend is rising). It now claims more lives than drink-driving and is one of the most common causes of accidents. People who use their smartphones in road traffic are generally considered road hogs. They are also pejoratively referred to as "smombies" (= "smartphone" + "zombies").

Stop it! Digital Detox is the name of the trend that reduces the use of electronic devices to a minimum and ensures more deceleration in everyday life. Simply switch off, turn it down, leave it at home - whatever the method, any form of time-out is welcome.

It's a paradox! Today we long for time more than ever. But our mobile phones, of all things, devour the most of it. Let's just switch it off or put it down for a while. A morning without an alarm clock is wonderful. A day without a mobile phone is a luxury: just look out of the window more often, watch the sky. Look into the eyes of the person you are talking to and enjoy the time together. Looking out of the window on the train and allowing yourself to daydream again. Enjoying dinner without push notifications and finally, finally not hearing any more pseudo-relevant news. And probably the email can wait until tomorrow!

---

Sometimes you just have to stay in bed. With the amount of sleep we usually get, every extra hour is probably good for us. Many of us suffer from a chronic lack of sleep. Lying down not only relaxes our muscles, skeleton and back. Our minds, too often preoccupied with too many things, also relax. Sufficient sleep also sharpens our mind. Those who get enough sleep are wide awake afterwards, are better able to cope with complex tasks and are prepared to think longer and more thoroughly about a matter before deciding for or against something. Our senses are sharpened and we are better able to absorb, comprehend and process new things.

It is even believed that sleep helps us lose weight. The reason for this is probably that we cannot eat at the same time while we sleep. No, all joking aside! It has been proven that digestion is stimulated during sleep. This continuously burns fat and releases the body's own hormones that suppress the feeling of hunger. If we sleep badly, this natural process is switched off and we are overcome by a feeling of hunger at night.

As soon as I am on holiday, I banish all watches and alarm clocks. I don't make appointments in the morning so I don't have to be artificially woken up. Of course, I don't sleep until eleven every day. I usually wake up on my own between eight and ten o'clock, so I usually sleep for eight to nine hours. But even if it's ten o'clock sometimes - what's the big deal? On holiday, you're allowed to sleep in sometimes!

For me, sleep is always like a little journey into nirvana. At least that's how I imagine the state before and after life. In between lies sleep - a kind of nocturnal excursion there. And honestly, that's not bad, is it? In nothingness I have nothing to do, nothing to think about, nothing to have to do. Nothing hurts, one is neither hungry nor thirsty nor tired - just completely relaxed - a kind of primal state. Sinking into nothingness. So why the guilty conscience?

But rarely does nothingness remain. Sleep also includes dreaming. When we dream, our soul undertakes interesting journeys to interesting places. I virtually experience dream journeys. Of course, one wonders what they could mean. There are numerous attempts at explanation on the part of dream interpretation. But I distrust them. There are even places in my dreams to which I return again and again. Places that do not exist in reality. And then there are the nights when you just can't fall asleep. Those are the ones when the moon is full. Scientists have found that less melatonin is produced on full moon nights. Melatonin is a messenger substance that controls the sleep-wake rhythm (the "inner clock").

But the nights after exhausting days are particularly difficult. If I haven't been out in the fresh air and haven't exercised much, the night literally turns into day. The thoughts circle and the day repeats itself involuntarily in my head. But there are strategies that can help: One of them is to accept the condition! If I know in advance that the night will be short, I can adjust to it and say, "Oh yes, I'm definitely not going to sleep a wink again today. That's okay. I've been there before. The next day might not be so nice, but I'll get through it somehow (with a few more cups of coffee if necessary)". Instead, I think about what I could do with the sleepless night. I read or listen to an audio book, and if I take it easy like that, I sometimes get surprised by my sudden tiredness and fall asleep quickly. Another helpful method is intense exercise! The rule is: the more strenuous the day, the more intense the workout. Up to two hours of jogging or strength training until exhaustion. This works wonders and creates a high sleep pressure that is difficult to escape. Other possibilities are taking food supplements such as magnesium or L-tryptophan (amino acid), keeping the room cool, sleeping with the window open or meditating.

# At least nine hours of sleep

As already mentioned, sufficient sleep plays a crucial role in well-being. Nine hours of sleep is ideal for me, but everyday life doesn't always allow for that, despite many minimalism measures. How some people can be satisfied with only six or seven hours of sleep, however, is a mystery to me. For me, that would clearly be giving up a piece of quality of life. Every hour that I don't sleep enough has a noticeably negative effect and not only leaves ugly circles under my eyes, but also puts me in a bad mood, leads to irritability, headaches and a constant feeling of hunger - all day long.

For me, holidays are first and foremost a time of rest and regeneration. Productivity can wait - right up until the moment when I am rested and ready for the challenges of the day. I am firmly convinced that the performance, balance, creativity and energy that is in all of us only comes out when we are also well-rested. All these positive aspects can only unfold during the recovery phases of sleep - and certainly not by interrupting sleep or even lack of sleep. That's why I banish the alarm clock from my free time. I'd rather turn over once more, collect myself and look forward to the day well rested.

I am aware that healthy and balanced sleep has a fundamental influence on my physical and mental health. During the night's rest, my cells regenerate, my brain processes the experiences of the day and my energy reserves are replenished. I have learned how important it is to give my body the time it needs to function optimally.

To further improve my sleep quality, I have developed various rituals and habits over time. It started with small changes in my sleeping environment. I transformed my bedroom into an oasis of relaxation and well-being. Soothing colours - such as white and beige bed linen - a pleasant room temperature, constant fresh air and a comfortable bed (in my case a harder mattress) all contribute to making me feel completely at ease and secure. The room is furnished in a very minimalist way. Decorative cushions, soft toys, ironing board, dressing table, storage boxes and everything else in the room I have removed, of course.

In addition, bedtime plays a crucial role for me. By consciously keeping a fixed sleep-wake rhythm, I have given my body a routine that helps it prepare for the sleep ahead. Regular bedtimes and a fixed routine before going to bed help me to get to sleep faster and wake up rested in the morning.

But despite all my efforts, there are days when sleep is not as restful as I would like. In such moments, I don't let frustration or anger get the better of me, but accept that sleep is not sleep. Instead, I use this time for myself to consciously listen to myself, sort out my thoughts and focus on what brings me joy.

Ultimately, I have come to realise that sleep is an essential part of physical and mental health and well-being. Many people are not always aware of this! Most people who crave a holiday really just need a capful of sleep. Maybe they don't know, maybe they're not supposed to know. Sometimes you're just in too deep or can't see the obvious anymore! Yet it can be so simple if you just allow yourself some rest and a few restful nights. Maybe the next long-distance trip will take care of it, who knows? I can only speak from my own experience: After a good night's sleep, I am deeply relaxed and blissful. Then I feel really good. I have no longings to satisfy, no deficits to make up for. Everything seems perfect just as it is! In such moments, I don't think about travelling at all. It's different when the tiredness lasts longer or after a strenuous week. Then you need a balance. Often you project your wishes onto a sun lounger by the sea, a swimming pool or a cruise - whatever - the main thing is to go far, far away! Advertising works! And the problem might be solved - but only maybe.

# Clean & comfortable

Lemons, peppermint oil, vinegar, rye flour, aloe vera, baking soda, coconut oil, olive oil and Aleppo soap - with these simple ingredients, the entire body care routine can be replaced naturally. At least partially, because the implementation takes time above all. It is fun to experiment with these simple products and discover what wonderful effects they can unfold. Liquid shampoo from the bottle, toothpaste or creams from the tube can be replaced by herbal alternatives, as they are in principle also "edible". That is the crucial difference!

I will explain what all this has to do with Holistay in the following. But first let's take a look at these products.

Rye flour

Instead of shampoo, you can wash your hair with rye flour, for example. Simply put some rye flour (please not the wholemeal variety) in a bowl, mix with lukewarm water until the mixture is creamy but not thick. It should look like almond milk, but not almond paste. Simply apply to damp hair, massage in, leave on for about two minutes and rinse. You just have to be careful not to get lumps in your hair, but that's rarely the case even with long hair like mine.

Strangely enough, only rye flour is suitable for this hair wash, no other grain product, neither oats, spelt nor wheat. Please do not experiment! I have heard all kinds of horror stories about it. Rye flour is odourless and can be diluted very well with water. Therefore, clogging of the sink is not to be feared. After drying (preferably in the air) you are amazed. The hair shines. When I use rye flour for the hair, however, I have the feeling that the hair becomes greasy again after about twelve hours. But maybe that's just a phase of getting used to it. My hair is used to being washed every day.

Lemon

What do we do with the lemon? Let's stay with the hair first. The lemon - or rather the juice of the lemon - is a natural remedy for lightening the hair. As soon as the sun shines, simply drizzle some lemon juice on your hair. Place in the sun for a few minutes and then rinse well. Each time you use it, your hair will become a little lighter without being damaged. Lemons are also great as a cleanser, sliced for a deliciously tasty refreshing drink (with a digestive effect) and diffused around the room for a lovely room fragrance.

And while we're at it: The fact that scents have a great influence on our well-being is an insight that does not have to be proven by scientific studies. There are scents that stimulate us, that calm us and that simply do us good. They have a direct effect on our limbic system and release happiness hormones. With high-quality essential oils from controlled organic cultivation, we can support this process. Whether orange, cinnamon, lavender, rose or sandalwood, tea tree or lemongrass - they all conjure up a pleasant atmosphere in our home. What we smell, we feel. This also explains certain preferences such as the scent of coffee or freshly mown grass or even the scent of lemon. We associate it with freshness, spring and cleanliness.

Coconut oil

Now we come to the next "all-rounder" - coconut oil. Coconut oil now replaces creams and cosmetics for me. Mixed with a little baking soda and peppermint oil, coconut oil can even be made into toothpaste. I use coconut oil in various dishes and drinks (e.g. tea and coffee). It replaces butter and frying fat. In the morning, coconut oil can be gently massaged under tired eyes, it also works great against dry skin and is suitable as an eye make-up remover and lip care.

I couldn't believe it myself, but together with baking soda, coconut oil works better than any deodorant: five kilometres of cycling, water bottles up to the fourth floor and another round of running in the evening. I worked up quite a sweat, but I didn't notice anything olfactory!

Baking soda

The already mentioned bicarbonate of soda is also a miracle cure. It is said to help against sweaty feet or bad breath. The white crystal salt has not only become known through the Zero Waste movement, but is a tried and tested and versatile household remedy that was already known to our grandmother. Sources prove its use already in ancient times.

Sodium bicarbonate is weakly alkaline and chemically known as sodium hydrogen carbonate ($NaHCO_3$). Not to be confused with sodium, caustic soda or caustic soda. The ancient Egyptians probably used sodium bicarbonate for ritual cleansing and later for mummification. In our country, it is more commonly known as a food additive, baking or cooking agent. Sodium bicarbonate replaces baking powder, deacidifies food, helps with heartburn and softens vegetables more quickly when cooking. It is also a component of many mineral and medicinal waters. In addition to its odour-neutralising properties, it can also be used as a fabric softener, cleaning agent or effective stain remover. It is a true all-rounder and is sometimes called baking powder, bicarbonate of soda or emperor's soda.

Aleppo soap

Let's move on to the soaps, especially Aleppo soap, a laurel soap from Syria that is one of my favourites. Alternatively, of course, you can use the French variant Savon or a simple olive oil soap. What I particularly like about Aleppo soap is not only its earthy scent, but also its creamy consistency, which is great for skin care. Unlike many other soaps, it does not dry out the skin. It is excellent for shaving and removes all kinds of facial make-up in one go, even waterproof mascara or kohl.

Or curd soap: it's a cool alrounder and is also made of sodium bicarbonate. Many people are no longer familiar with it, but it is excellent for all household cleaning, window cleaning, laundry washing and even as a cleaning agent in the kitchen.

Aloe Vera

Now let's move on to my favourite plant, the aloe vera. The desert flower, also called the true aloe, lives up to its name. Even as a child, I came into contact with the healing power of this plant without really understanding what was going on. The gel-like substance that oozes from the leaves of the plant was applied to insect bites, grazes or sunburns, as it was said to strengthen the body's defences and have an antibacterial effect. The juice extracted from the plant can be prepared as a tea (helps e.g. with digestive problems and constipation) and is often used as a food supplement. Aloe vera belongs in every medicine cabinet and should therefore not be missing from any windowsill. It is a true multi-talent and can be used against headaches, gastrointestinal complaints, skin redness and blemishes or simply for skin care.

Peppermint oil

As mentioned earlier, you can make a natural toothpaste with some peppermint oil, baking soda and coconut oil. Peppermint oil, which is extracted from peppermint by steam distillation and is one of the essential oils, has many health benefits. For example, it can be used for headaches (by rubbing it lightly on the temples), respiratory problems (expectorant) or irritable bowel syndrome. And almost everyone likes the smell of mint. It is very stimulating, refreshing and at the same time soothing.

The use of peppermint can also be traced back to ancient Egypt, where it was used in many ways. The plant, especially the leaves, has always been considered a remedy. But it is only in the form of oil that peppermint unfolds its special health-promoting effect: it relaxes the muscles, aids digestion and clears the respiratory tract. The ingredients menthol and menthone have a cooling and antibacterial effect. They have an analgesic effect and are therefore very effective for headaches. Peppermint oil can be applied directly to the skin (but be careful not to get it in the eye area) and inhaled with hot water vapour.

Vinegar

Finally, let's take a look at vinegar: Shower cubicles, kettles, coffee machines, cutlery, glasses and taps are often affected by limescaleThis not only doesn't look nice, but also leads to damage to the appliances in the long run. Thanks to a vinegar treatment (simply put some vinegar on a sponge, rub the affected area with it, let it work for a few minutes and then rinse it off with lukewarm water), these parts look like new again - and this is not a publicity stunt, but a fact that is unfortunately unknown to many. Vinegar is an effective means of bringing even the shabbiest metal and glass back to a high shine. Simple, inexpensive and fast!

So, enough cleaning. We don't want to spend too much time on it in our free time, do we? Yet cleanliness is an important part of the recovery process - in many ways. If you keep your home clean, you feel good all around and recover faster. Cleaning can even be fun, especially if you see results quickly. I find it a meditative task to mop the floor by hand (I don't have a hoover, of course). You learn a lot about mindfulness and stay fit and active along the way.

Cleanliness means stress relief. Just washing the dishes, hanging up the laundry or making the bed fresh can have an immediate positive effect on the psyche. It's just a great feeling when everything smells so fresh and clean. When we tidy and sort, something serious also happens in our minds: we let go and bring about direct change. We actively shape our environment. We ourselves contribute to making it nicer and cosier. And who doesn't enjoy coming home after a hard day's work, taking a shower, slipping into clean clothes and lying down in a freshly made bed? That's how we feel when we travel. It's a nice moment to enter the hotel room and find a tidy room. It's the perfect start to a holiday - and that's how Holistay should be every day! It's nice to come home and find a clean, beautiful flat. The end of the day can begin.

For that to happen, regular decluttering - letting go of things we no longer need and that are just getting in the way - is certainly part of the process.

Strictly speaking, it is not customary to wash dishes, sweep the floor, take out the rubbish or clean the toilet while on holiday. But precisely because everything is so minimalist and manageable, these tasks almost take care of themselves. I don't plan any extra hours to clean and tidy up the flat. Everything goes by the way and without much effort. I make the bed as soon as I get up, I wash the dishes immediately after using them, I take the rubbish with me when I go out the door anyway, and the two deposit bottles are in my bag because I'm sure to pass a supermarket. So cleaning becomes a small meditative sideline rather than a chore.

# Places where the soul travels

There are still places where you start dreaming and travelling as soon as you enter. These include libraries, bookshops, second-hand bookshops, some new business concepts (e.g. concept stores), festivals, art exhibitions, museums and even flea markets. These places are ideal for finding inspiration, for a new direction of thought or for a journey into the past.

I have discovered the fascinating world of books for myself (or rather, I enjoy the company of individual authors and their ideas). Books can motivate, abduct, educate, enlighten, inspire, convince and enchant. They give a completely new view of the world. My life used to be often monotonous, but books have unexpectedly opened up new worlds for me that I would never have entered otherwise.

If I hadn't encountered Fontane, Goethe, Frisch, Kafka or Hesse in my youth, my life would probably have been very different and my view of the world would have been different.

Books were my teachers and my source of inspiration, even though I didn't understand everything back then. In German class we read the classics. We leafed through the little yellow Reclam books, marked important passages and discussed them together. I probably didn't realise it at the time, but it made me think. I am very grateful to the German school system for that today!

When I was a teenager, I liked going to the public library. I felt comfortable there. There were cosy sofa corners, games, a CD player and some computers with internet access. My library was in the middle of the high-rise housing estate where I grew up. My parents both worked from dawn to dusk, and my older sister took care of my little brother and me. So the library was a good refuge in the afternoons when you didn't know what to do with yourself.

Maybe that was one of the reasons why I decided to study humanities after school. Reading made me curious about life.

To this day, regular visits to the city library are among my favourite rituals. Even getting there puts me in high spirits: I stroll through a street lined with tall trees along the tram tracks that Bernhard Schlink described so beautifully in his book "The Reader" (1995). After crossing the large ring of streets, I arrive directly at the meadow with the almond trees. Once a year, in spring, they blossom in full splendour and give the small green spot directly in front of the Heidelberg public library an almost fairytale-like setting. In the library, I pass children playing, pensioners reading the newspaper and students working on their laptops. I look for the aisle with my favourite literature and browse through the rows of books. After a short while, I find the right book and sit down directly in front of the shelf on the carpeted floor. I delve into travel literature, psychological works or medical guides. Next to me, books pile up that I absolutely have to read - sometimes there are three, sometimes ten. But every now and then I just pick up a magazine. Then I go to the café next door and enjoy the time. The magic of my childhood library can still be felt today. No sooner have I read a few lines than I'm already in a whole other world.

And this is how the magic works: I hold the book in my hands and look at its cover for a moment. Then I turn it over and read the spine attentively. Carefully I study the table of contents. The information about the author also plays a big role for me. I always want to know who I am dealing with. Who is this person I am paying attention to? What motivated him to write this book? What experiences has he had, what does he have to tell me? What can I draw from this for myself personally?

Then I flip to the first pages, to the table of contents. Here I decide whether to continue reading the book. The first sentences of the introduction are very important. They give me an impression of what is to come. Sometimes authors have the ability to immediately draw me in so that I can't put the book down. Authors not only become my "friends" in a figurative sense, but more importantly, they become my mentors and maybe even my role models! Occasionally, I even get in touch with some of them to express my appreciation or thanks or to get them for an expert interview on my blog. I have already met fascinating people this way. Reading them enriches me a lot! Of course, I won't be able to talk to everyone, but the works usually speak for themselves. And everyone usually draws their own message from literature! Sometimes I only understand them many years later (as was the case with the books from my school days), and then in a very concrete way!

When I've finished the introduction, I often do something unusual, almost comical. I turn the book over and flip through it from back to front - quite differently than usual, as if it were a Japanese or Arabic edition. I don't know exactly why I do this, but I love flipping through books from back to front. Of course, I also look at the illustrations if there are any. But the best books are the ones that stimulate the imagination and create your own pictures in your head.

# Put away the camera, bring on the pens!

On my travels, I once made an amazing and, to some, perhaps crazy-sounding decision: I stopped taking photographs. At first it may seem unusual, but this choice has turned out to be a liberating experience. In the past, I was always busy taking countless photos on holiday - much like Chinese tourists, whom we often smile about. A photo here, a photo there, but hardly any time to notice what is in front of the lens. At the end of a trip, I used to have tons of picture material, often even the same motif from different perspectives. That was not only time-consuming, but also quite boring. The more pictures I had, the less I looked at them in the end. I realised that something had to change.

Now, when I'm out and about, I look very closely and try to perceive the moment with all my senses. I even stop for ten minutes if I have to in order to consciously look at a landscape that I find beautiful at the moment - without taking pictures. Now, when I'm on the road, I consciously take time for my surroundings. I try not to lose myself in the world of photography, but to engage fully with the beauty of the place. Instead of constantly looking through the lens of my camera, I look at the landscapes, sights and people in peace.

## Photos - not always important

Some people would literally go crazy if they couldn't capture everything on camera. Especially when it comes to holidays or special events, people want to make sure that they remain unforgettable. For some, the motto is: "What wasn't photographed or filmed didn't happen". A photo of the moment gives a sense of material reality. It gives some a good feeling to be able to look at the picture later and share them with friends through social media channels. In the age of smartphones, everyone always has a camera at hand. Everyone becomes a photographer of their own life. This is how more and more pictures are created that tell us: "I was there. I experienced it. This moment is a part of me and here is the proof". Perhaps it is also a small feeling of power, a securing and storing of memory, perhaps combined with the fear of forgetting (becoming). How can we be sure that we will still remember this situation in ten years if there are no pictures? Can we really trust our memory? And how can we share our experiences with friends and family if we can't show them pictures? Would we also be able to put our experiences into words without pictorial support and without forgetting an important detail? In fact, many people have difficulty with this. And of course, memories fade after a few years, maybe even get mixed up with other memories or partially forgotten. Many people feel insecure about this issue.

But if we are honest, we never look at most of the photos again. In the meantime, thousands of superfluous pictures have been created. It is incredibly time-consuming to sort through them. To recall and relive old memories again and again. Moreover, many photos do not correspond to reality. They are posed or show trivialities like street facades, house walls or meals that are not really worth remembering.

Moreover, we must not forget: We only capture a tiny moment torn out of an action, including the mood, the smells, the sounds, the atmosphere and the context. In a sense, we "petrify" reality in this one image, making it a lasting memory that stands like a monument to the whole situation. But we only have a fraction of the whole in view, which must be reinterpreted by us in each case. A handful of photos becomes the support of our memory, on which we rely more and more. We also spend a lot of time leafing through our past, sometimes forgetting that the present is also beautiful.

There is nothing wrong with having photos from the past if they give us positive feelings and make us happy in the present. Photos are great for this purpose. But we quickly miss the special moments that we can't and don't need to capture. We no longer really look, but only at the screen. Just going to a concert without filming half the evening is great too. The same goes for a visit to the zoo: just watch the birds, feed the carp, observe the butterflies and have a picnic, without panoramic photos or animal portraits that nobody wants to look at anymore anyway.

Less is more - of course photos of the prom, your own wedding or a special outing are important and great. But do you really have to capture every visit to a restaurant, every flower bed and every funny grimace of your children with your camera? Which photos are really important?

---

This change has taken my travel experience to a whole new level. I now feel much more connected to the places I visit. My memories are not just photos, but deep memories because I consciously experienced those moments. Enjoying the sunset, seeing people laughing, watching the colourful hustle and bustle on the streets - all this is now in my memory, not in the photo.

By freeing myself from the urge to take the next snapshot, I live completely in the here and now. Instead of constantly looking for the perfect photo, I can just surrender to the moment and let the experience wash over me. I no longer feel driven to capture every moment, but can simply enjoy the beauty and uniqueness of the moment.

You can go one step further and resolve to draw beautiful moments from now on. Provided, of course, that you know how to use a pen. So why not capture the most beautiful memories creatively? It offers a longer occupation with the motif, is a lot of fun, also has a meditative character and is really something special.

A self-painted holiday memory is really something special and remains in the memory forever or perhaps even finds a place of honour on the wall. You can also have yourself painted (if you are not artistically talented yourself).

# Sleeping in broad daylight

Yes, the topic of sleep is once again in the spotlight. This time it's about the midday nap, the siesta, a real luxury that few people allow themselves (especially not full-time employees). In reality, there are hardly any opportunities for retreat and the work environment often disapproves of such breaks. After all, no one wants to be caught closing their eyes for a moment at work and taking a snooze. And it would certainly look funny if we just lay down on a park bench and take a nap.

As tempting as the nap may be, it remains a pipe dream for now - unless we're on holiday, it's the weekend or we have a few days off. A trend from the USA could soon change that: There are more and more so-called sleep cafés. There, guests can not only drink coffee, but also take a nap. What a wonderful idea: pillows instead of caffeine. When will it also be here with us?

Especially in summer, when the temperatures rise, a longer lunch break makes sense. We already know this concept from warm countries around the Mediterranean. There, the traditional siesta takes place: people retire at noon to become active again in the evening.

# Water makes you thirsty for holidays

For us, vacations and water are often inextricably linked - whether it's a picturesque lake, a tranquil river, an idyllic bathing bay, a swimming pool or the endless sea. In my current hometown, located directly on the beautiful Neckar River, I can feel this connection particularly well. Every time I walk along the banks of the Neckar and cross the bridges, I am filled with a pleasant vacation mood. In the past, it was the Pegnitz in Nuremberg or the Queich in Landau. Every walk along the water is like a little vacation for me. Especially on hot summer days, the water is a welcome cooling. You can put your feet in the water, rent a pedal boat or a canoe, take a relaxing boat ride, and - if you're lucky - even go swimming.

During my time in Nuremberg, I made a joyful surprise one day while jogging. I discovered a swimming lake, which I had not known until then. The temperatures were unbearably high that day. So the cooling off came just in time. Without hesitation, I decided to jump into the clear water of the lake. Fortunately, I had anyway a pair of shorts and a sports bra on, which can also be worn well as a bikini. After all, I was not the only swimmer! It was unforgettable and really fun. This unexpected discovery was like a little vacation adventure! From then on, the bathing lake became my permanent destination whenever I felt like a refreshing break in the summer.

The calming effect of water, the cooling on hot days, the gentle lapping, the immersion under water, the expansive view - all this nourishes our soul and gives us precious moments of happiness.

Whether walking along a riverbank, dipping your feet in a refreshing lake, or gliding across the water in a boat, water has the wonderful ability to relax, to refresh, to remind you of a vacation. These are the small pleasures of daily life, because rivers, lakes and bathing bays are everywhere. Water thus becomes a daily source of relaxation and sometimes inspiration. Because it always immediately puts me in a vacation mood, no matter where I am.

# Reading a philosophical book

"Who, how, what? Why, why, why?" - Every child knows the opening melody of "Sesamstrasse" - the most successful television series for pre-schoolers in Germany - and it could well be considered the first encounter with philosophy. After all, these are the central questions that mankind has been dealing with since time immemorial. For a long time, these questions were answered primarily by religions. Certainly, it is fascinating what the gods have to say about it. But as the saying goes, "He who does not ask remains stupid!" So let us turn to philosophy. It deals with the basic questions of being. The doctrine of such not directly experienceable things is called "metaphysics". But it is less about explaining supposed supernatural powers, gods or a life after death. Rather, philosophy differs from theology precisely in that it pursues a purely intellectual approach to the object of investigation, for example by applying logic.

Thales of Miletus (ca. 624 to 548 BC), the first "philosophical thinker" known to us, encouraged people to fathom the essence of things with the help of reason. Later, Immanuel Kant, in his famous Critique of Pure Reason, urged people to courageously use their own reason ("sapere aude!").

Philosophy is not only about abstract questions of being, origin and meaning. We all practice philosophy to a greater or lesser extent as soon as we deal with questions of everyday life.

Philosophy can be called "Ars Vivendi", the science of the art of living.

The term philosophy basically reveals what it is all about: the love (Greek "philía") of wisdom (Greek "sophía"). At the beginning there is curiosity and the desire for a fulfilled and good life. As soon as we ask our questions reasonably, remain critical and do not allow ourselves to be determined by others, we find ourselves on philosophical terrain.

Unfortunately, in our often condensed or hectic daily lives, we rarely find the time to further sensitize and nurture our (critical) thinking. Especially today, with the advent of the Internet and the associated flood of information, critical questioning and the ability to distinguish truth from untruth are of great importance. Philosophy can help us with this. It provides us with a kind of bird's eye view, expands our horizons of knowledge and brings us closer to a life that is as self-determined and autonomous as possible and that corresponds to our ideal values. But philosophy is not only excellent for this.

The examination of philosophical ideas leads us to new, enriching, even electrifying thoughts that make us look at life from a completely new perspective. With representatives of the Stoa such as Epictetus, Seneca or Marcus Aurelius, for example, we can practice emotional self-control, which in everyday life means above all serenity and inner peace even in turbulent times. With Plato we find the way out of the shadowy existence. Those who want to put their own power of judgment to the test reach for Kant. With Nietzsche we overcome the traditional view of man. With him, the question arises as to what values such as morality, good and evil mean if we disregard God (and thus the Christian socialization of our society). Rousseau brings back the wisdom of nature, Sartre freedom, and de Beauvoir paves the way for equal rights for men and women.

Philosophy is not only the love of wisdom but also a journey to oneself. It helps us design inner maps - less in the form of stories and adventures, but more as puzzle pieces of our own life concept. Because one question keeps occupying us repeatedly: What is a happy life? What is the meaning of life? The next world trip is unlikely to answer these questions unless one takes ample time for philosophical contemplation.

The purpose of philosophy is not to soothe our conscience or to keep us from doing anything that gives us pleasure. Rather, it is to question certain desires and ideas that in reality are not always our own. This realization is invaluable! Many of our actions and thought patterns have been instilled in us throughout our lives, we have been socialized and strongly influenced by the society in which we live. It is not a matter of criticizing our view of experiences, possessions or opinions out of hand - rather, it is a matter of accepting what is and making life in the present as good as it can be.

That's why we should deal with philosophical thoughts as often as possible in Holistay. Because while many everyday situations often demotivate or wear us down, philosophical ideas give us new courage. Philosophy frees us from imposed thought patterns and inspires us to think outside the box. Where am I right now? Why am I doing what I am doing? What is behind it? These questions open up new perspectives and help us to shape our lives more consciously.

Philosophy helps people to reflect on themselves and to question their place in the world again and again. It can provide comfort in times of grief and proves to be a reliable source of serenity in emotionally upsetting moments. But it also requires a willingness to see the mundane in a new light again and again, and to give our lives a new direction if necessary. Philosophy can be understood as an entrance ticket into our own world of thoughts and is thus the best way to Holistay. It is worthwhile to explore one's own self with curiosity and openness.

Here are some book recommendations for getting started with philosophy:

- *At The Existentialist Café: Freedom, Being, and Apricot Cocktails* by Sarah Bakewell (2017)
- *Philosophy 101: From Plato and Socrates to Ethics and Metaphysics, an Essential Primer on the History of Thought* by Paul Kleinman (2013)
- *The Daily Stoic: 366 Meditations on Wisdom, Perseverance, and the Art of Living* by Ryan Holiday (2017)
- *50 Philosophy Classics: Thinking, Being, Acting Seeing – Profound Insights and Powerful Thinking from Fifty Key Books* by Tom Butler Bowdon (2013)
- *Humankind: A Hopeful History* by Rudger Bregman (2020)
- *Meditations: New Translation (Modern Library Classics)* by Marcus Aurelius (author) Gregory Hays (translator) (2003)
- *Who Am I and If So How Many? A Journey Through Your Mind* by Richard David Precht (2011)
- *Nasty, Brutish, and Short: Adventures in Philosophy* by Scott Hershovitz (2022)

# Places where body and mind can truly rest

This year I wanted something completely different for my birthday: no flowers, no jewellery and certainly no cake. I didn't want to have a party, go out to eat or go on a trip. This time I just wanted a day pass for the Premium Fitness Studio. When it comes to sports, I'm not usually a big fan of "mucking out". I prefer to be out in the fresh air. But for a wellness break in between, the premium fitness studios are definitely worth a visit.

Most gyms in the upper price range have a great sauna area where you can go after sweating on the treadmill, strength training on the machines or an hour of Pilates. I really wanted to try this out on my birthday. I wanted to do something good for my body, first really work out on the machines and then relax in the wellness area. Instead of getting a year older, you feel 10 years younger. That's a good trade-off, isn't it?

It's worth finding out in which gym this is possible. Sometimes really beautiful sauna landscapes are hidden behind the doors, just waiting to be discovered.

To be best prepared for a day at the gym, you should bring the following things: clean trainers, suitable sportswear and enough water. It is advisable to bring at least three towels: a small one for the equipment, a large one for the sauna and one to dry off after showering. Don't forget shower gel, bathing shoes, fresh underwear and enough time!

Of course, a fitness and wellness day like this is not only suitable for a birthday, but also for any holiday. Others book expensive club hotels abroad with wellness facilities that they share with hundreds of guests and may not always be able to use to the full. I prefer the gym around the corner, which I can reach quickly and visit more often. The gym is also the perfect place on rainy afternoons. What could be better than sweating in the sauna while it's pouring outside?

Speaking of hotels: The local hotels also have such offers and sometimes offer them to out-of-town guests. In Nuremberg, for example, there is the five-star Sheraton Carlton Hotel directly at the main railway station. Visitors pay a fee of about 15 euros and can use the sauna, the whirlpool and the small gym. The best thing about it is the breathtaking view of the castle and the roofs of the city. In Heidelberg, it's the Hotel Europäischer Hof that offers sports, beauty and wellness for out-of-town visitors.

Somewhere nearby there is bound to be a modern bathing facility, a thermal bath, a salt grotto or a wellness park? Just google it and try it out. Even if some wellness facilities seem very artificial, they often offer a relaxing atmosphere where you can rest and switch off for a few hours in between.

# A massage for your ears

Talking about wellness: Who doesn't like to get a massage? Massages are important and beneficial because they have many positive effects on body and mind. They help to relieve muscle tension, promote blood circulation and thus contribute to the more efficient distribution of nutrients and oxygen in the body and the faster removal of waste products. Massages can loosen hardened muscles and relieve pain caused, for example, by incorrect posture or too much strain. Of course, massages reduce stress hormones and promote general well-being. And when we massage each other - touch each other - we strengthen our interpersonal relationships.

And this brings us to the problem: in our society, "touching" is not so far off. This has something to do with our cultural norms, which determine what is appropriate. Of course, everyone has individual touch preferences and limits. Most people feel uncomfortable being touched by others, even if it is meant lovingly. Many people also do not have much experience with massage or conscious touch and are therefore unsure how to do it properly. Many are also afraid of misunderstandings or misinterpretations. While physiotherapy is becoming more and more common, massage by a partner after a hard day's work is rather rare in our country.

I worked in a fashion shop for a short time. We had many elderly customers. Often they needed help getting dressed. I helped them to get their arm into the blouse or jacket. I pulled up their back zip or wrapped the matching scarf around their neck. Many gladly took advantage of this service. But of course, very few of these customers really needed a new wardrobe. They had full wardrobes at home. Rather, they were looking for communication and human closeness, gentle touches, hugs or just a smile. We knew that and they were, after all, our best clientele.

And now to the ears - a part of the body that is often underestimated in our Western society, but which can be positively stimulated in a wonderful way through massage. Traditional Chinese Medicine (TCM) is quite different: Here, the ear is considered an important body region with numerous acupuncture points and reflex zones that are said to be connected to various organs and body parts. Ear massage or ear acupressure is a sub-area of ear acupuncture or auriculotherapy in TCM. The so-called Shen Men point, which is located above the auricle at the end of the large arch fold, is even said to help directly against migraines and stress when touched and gently massaged. After just a few minutes of massage at this point, there is a clear improvement in well-being.

In TCM, the ear symbolises a body turned 90 degrees in the foetal position. The earlobe represents the head, the outer arch represents the spine and inside the ear are the heart, lungs and internal organs. Further up the ear are the legs, and the tip of the ear represents the coccyx. Although the ear only occupies a small area, it represents the whole body. And the effect of massage at this point is impressive. Ear massage can relieve many ailments. These include migraines, fatigue and digestive problems, but also stress, appetite and sleep disorders. TCM emphasises the importance of the energy pathways in the body and their influence on our health. By stimulating these reflex zones, the flow of energy (Qi) is supposed to be harmonised and well-being promoted. In addition to the reflex zones, there are also specific acupuncture points that can be stimulated. These points are assigned to the meridians and organ systems of the body. Through ear massage, these energy pathways can be stimulated and blockages can be released.

Ear massages are a wonderful way to integrate wellness into everyday life without having to rely on expensive masseurs or exotic holidays. You can use this simple technique at any time to do yourself some good. Massage is simply part of the holistay!

Culture and nature -
right in front of the door

# Solo and in good company

Those who spend their holidays at home have a lot of free time. Often one spends this time alone. One is not lonely, but consciously spends time with oneself. There is a big difference between the terms "loneliness" and "being alone". Aloneness refers to a state in which a person is physically or emotionally separated from other people. Aloneness is usually chosen voluntarily. It is often seen as a time of rest, retreat and self-reflection, a deliberate time to oneself in which to gather one's thoughts, relax or pursue one's personal interests. It can be seen as a positive and necessary experience to get to know oneself better and to appreciate one's independence. Loneliness is something quite different: it is the feeling of emotional isolation that can arise when a person has a need for social connections and emotional closeness, but feels that these needs are not being met. For this reason, loneliness can occur both in the presence and absence of other people. It is a subjective feeling of emptiness, sadness or frustration due to a lack of social support or connectedness.

Here, being alone is deliberately meant: Why not consciously use the holiday at home to go into oneself, gather, relax and pursue one's personal interests in peace?

Holistay is a journey to oneself. Finally, you have time to deal with what's on your mind. You find out what happiness means to you personally or what you are fundamentally missing to be happy.

In order to diversify this special time with yourself, activities such as drawing, writing, listening to music, maybe also handicrafts, baking and of course the classic philosophising and meditating are suitable. But outdoor activities such as hiking, jogging and cycling are also a must.

By giving yourself and your thoughts space, you gain a deeper understanding of what is really important to you. This self-reflection is especially important at a time when we are constantly faced with decisions. At the same time, it strengthens self-confidence, promotes inner serenity and gives us decisive advantages for future challenges. As we get older, for example, it can become more difficult to make new friends or maintain existing relationships. Nowadays, we are all very busy and unfortunately miss many valuable opportunities to meet and spend beautiful moments together. But the good news is: during the Holistay, this can no longer happen! On holiday at home - with more time in your luggage - you pay much more attention to what happens in everyday life. You are more spontaneous, try something new more often and find time for all the nice things you would otherwise have to cancel. But Holistay has even more advantages!

People who travel far away often rave about meeting great people, having a good time together and making good friends. These are, of course, convincing arguments to pack our bags and set off into the wide world. But can't we do exactly that here locally? How can we, for example, get to know new people in our surroundings and neighbourhood? Why does that sometimes seem so difficult and complicated? And what do we do differently when we are on the road?

Places where people usually make new acquaintances are clubs, adult education centres, pubs, parties and the workplace. But contacts can also be made in a queue, on a park bench, during a train journey or even while jogging. Every time you meet strangers, a conversation can start. At the checkout in the supermarket, for example, you can ask for an opinion or experience about a product. On a park bench, you can ask about the book the person is holding. The best way to get to know neighbours is in the lift, at the letterbox or in the laundry room. Maybe the neighbour will accept the parcel - a good opportunity to start a conversation.

Interestingly, sports, especially jogging, always provide good opportunities for small talk. Be it while stretching on the bridge or during a short breather. Sport is also always a good and innocuous topic of conversation. You can ask about shoes (ask for a recommendation), about the running route, about running groups, about the next running event or about the next water fountain.

Typical topics for starting a conversation with strangers are, of course, always the weather, traffic when the opportunity arises, questions about directions, recommendable restaurants or nice cafés and, of course, the sights of the city.

And why is it apparently always a little easier to meet new people on holiday? The trick to making fast acquaintances while travelling is that you often behave quite differently in foreign places: In other places you feel free, unobserved and relaxed. Alcohol often plays a role in loosening up the situation. On holiday, the rules are different. Here you can embarrass yourself less because you don't know each other. That is a big advantage! On holiday, we are often hyper. The many new experiences and impressions in a short time intoxicate us and release adrenaline. We are excited, our heart beats faster, we approach strangers more easily and fun is always in the foreground.

But ultimately it comes down to the inner attitude. Mindfulness, cheerfulness, genuine interest, joie de vivre, curiosity are not bound to certain places, times or people, but must be lived and practised at all times. The better we succeed in this in everyday life, the more cheerful our lives become. Then we don't need a plane ticket, a tropical climate and certainly no alcohol. Instead, we can lead a happy home life from now on.

# Learning new languages with Tandem

Travelling, they say, broadens the horizon. People also hope that a trip to foreign countries will refresh their own language skills. But if you really want to brush up or improve your language skills, you should spend more than just two weeks abroad. Perhaps one should even attend a language course and actively engage with the local population.

It is obvious that a language must be used regularly in everyday life in order to master it. A short holiday is not enough for this. Holistay, on the other hand, offers optimal conditions for continuous engagement with a foreign language and is generally ideal for lifelong learning.

Of course, I also want to brush up on my English regularly. There are many ways to do this in my free time. For example, you can attend a language course, either at an adult education centre or at a private educational institution. Individual lessons or the use of language learning apps and e-learning courses are also helpful options. It is also worth watching films and series in the foreign language or reading magazines, books, blogs and news in English. You can sing your favourite songs with subtitles or go to regulars' tables where people speak in the language.

I chose a tandem programme that I found on the internet. I find it easier to learn languages when I meet real people and can communicate with them face to face. And a tandem programme is wonderful for that: First, I registered online on a university platform, gave my name, age, place of residence, hobbies and the language I wanted, and the search for a suitable counterpart began. After a short time, I was introduced to a young woman of my age who lives near me. She comes from India, from Goa to be precise.

Immediately afterwards, we arranged to meet in a café to communicate for an hour in each other's languages. First we spoke in English, then in German. It didn't always quite work out, but it was fun. At some point, I only spoke in English and she answered me in German. That's how it worked best! Neither during her studies at a German university nor at her work in an international company does the trained engineer have to speak German. That's why she never really learned it, even though she has lived here for many years. Now she wants to catch up.

The nice thing about the language tandem programme is that you don't just learn the language, but with a bit of luck also nice people and their culture. We discussed cultural peculiarities and characteristics and quickly realised that we have a lot in common, be it our attitudes towards work-life balance, today's working world or our hobbies. She speaks fluent English, Konkani, Marati and Hindi. I was surprised to learn that she is also fluent in Portuguese and a devout Catholic. From her, I learned that the small state of Goa (on the west coast of India) was a Portuguese colony for almost 500 years and that is why the European influences are still so strong. The capital of Goa, Panaji, is very similar to Lisbon.

My new language friend is enthusiastic about Germany. She appreciates the change of the four seasons, loves the winter and the short distances. In contrast, Goa has a tropical climate with constant temperatures between 25 and 30 degrees Celsius. In the summer months of June and July, Goa is in monsoon season with frequent rainy days. My language partner is also enthusiastic about the working conditions in Germany. She can work from home for the most part, receives funding for further training and has significantly more holiday days than in her home country.

Goa, of course, has a lot to offer. With an area of over 3,700 square kilometres and a population of at least 1.5 million people, there is much to discover. Goa is characterised by its location on the Arabian Sea and a coastline of over 100 kilometres. About 40 per cent of the land is covered by greenery, including mango trees, banana trees, pineapple fields, jackfruit and sage trees, coconut palms, bamboo, ferns and orchids.

Leopards, parrots and cobras live in the forests of Goa. Compared to other Indian states, Goa has a good infrastructure and a comprehensive education system that enables many people to attend university. More than half of the population works in the service sector, e.g. banking, insurance or real estate.

Personally, I know Goa only from the origin story of the travel guide Lonely Planet (at that time I wrote my thesis on tourism, religion and marketing): Goa was a popular destination for backpackers on the so-called hippie trail from Europe to South Asia in the 1960s. What many don't know: Goa is a melting pot of religions. During the Portuguese rule, many people converted to Christianity. Today Goa is an Indian state where Christianity, Hinduism and other religions live peacefully together. And today Goa stands above all for its endless beaches, for its vibrant nightlife and for its festival scene.

I'm happy that I was not only able to brush up on my English skills through the language program, but above all learned something about a country that was previously foreign to me, made a new friend, and all that without having been iced out myself.

# Animals as friends

Recently, on my way home, I met a man with his white poodle. I knew neither dog nor master. When the poodle saw me, he suddenly stopped, sat down and looked at me. His master pulled the leash in amazement and for a moment did not know what was going on with his dog. Did he need to relieve himself or did he just want to rest? Then he also noticed my presence and turned back to his dog. We had to laugh. "He hasn't done anything like that yet," he said. We chatted briefly, I petted the four-legged friend and moved on. The poodle also continued on its way as if nothing had happened.

In my neighborhood there are many stray cats. These are well-kept and vaccinated house cats with free access. Especially in the evening I often meet them. They often lie lazily on the walls or curiously roam the streets. When we meet, I sometimes stroke their heads, especially if we already know each other and have crossed paths several times. Cats are known to have a fixed territory, which they regularly roam, control and defend if necessary. Rarely two cats share the same territory. Since I don't know their real names given to them by their owners, I simply invent new ones. For example, I call them Mitzi, Cleopatra, Lilli and Puma. I often meet them while jogging. Then I brake and stop briefly to say hello. After all, we've already become good friends.

In Heidelberg, we not only have dogs and cats, but also many birds right on our doorstep. One particular species of bird that lives here is the bright green collared parakeet. Originally, the bird probably comes from Africa - or so it is said - but apparently escaped from a private household and has multiplied diligently over decades. It obviously feels at home here in our forests and in the middle of the city. The collared parakeets have even settled in the entire Rhine region, including Mainz, Cologne and Düsseldorf. In Heidelberg, the feathered residents have been part of the cityscape for years. With their green plumage and red beak, they are not only eye-catching, but also hard to miss.

And if you go for a walk along the Neckar, you should have a look at the ducks. They are really entertaining. Ducks are water birds that exist everywhere except in Antarctica. They even feel at home in tropical rainforests. The female is spotted brown, the drake has a blue-green head. Ducks are diurnal and nocturnal, but above all they are migratory birds. They leave us in autumn and return only in spring. But when they are here, you should not miss this pleasure. For series lovers, this daily soap is an absolute must: ducks usually travel in pairs. The female leads, waddling curiously and hungrily - a true diva. The drake follows dutifully, vigilantly watching for possible danger and rivals. It looks funny when they paddle in the water with their hind legs to move forward. While the female calmly preens her plumage, he nervously makes his rounds, acting macho. His loud croaking is unmistakable and the courtship rituals during the mating season draws every attention. You could watch them for hours.

Then there is Atman, the little dog in the yard, whom I pass every day. He is very trusting and often waits by the wayside as if he had only one (life) task: to get a few strokes from passers-by and to make them laugh with his playful nature. So also me regularly.

In the summer months of June and July, you can observe something fascinating near bodies of water, on wet meadows, in bushes or in forest clearings. Small, green glowing fireflies fly through the air. For a long time I thought they only existed in fairy tales or dreams, like elves, goblins and dwarfs. But they really exist! You can imagine how surprised I was when I saw them in reality for the first time. I was invited that evening to a garden party at a friend's house, whose apartment is right on top of a hill in the Schlierbach district. As it started to get dark, we made a campfire, unpacked the guitar and snuggled under the warm blankets. Suddenly I saw green lights flying around in the garden and wasn't sure if someone might have poured something into my glass. "There are no fireflies," I said to my neighbor in amazement. Am I hallucinating?

Later at home, of course, I did some research: fireflies are normal beetles that have luminescent organs and use them when mating. They glow to attract potential mates. Through a biochemical reaction (the enzyme luciferase reacts with oxygen and adenosine triphosphate, or ATP - ATP is the energy carrier and regulator in our cells), energy is produced in the form of light. Since the rear end of the beetles is transparent, this light is visible in the dark.

Thus, beetles in love recognize each other better in the dark. That's the sober explanation, it's still kind of romantic!

Everywhere we live, we can meet the most diverse animals. Some see squirrels, hedgehogs and horses, others sheep, donkeys and foxes. Still others have deer, rabbits and butterflies around them. Many animals live peacefully and unobtrusively near us. They do us good and bring us a bit closer to nature again. We don't have to keep or own animals, but we should care for their welfare and integrity. Animals are our neighbors and our friends. They contribute to a peaceful coexistence and to a relaxed and fulfilled life.

# Outdoor sports

As a child, I was very active by nature and enjoyed being outside and moving around. I spent countless hours outdoors with my neighborhood friends. In the winter, we'd get our sleds out of the basement and sled down the hill; in the summer, water guns and games at the lake provided lots of fun. The weather didn't matter - rain or shine, we always had a great time outdoors and exercise was just always part of it.

When I started school, my relationship with sports changed. The institutionalized physical education classes at school weren't very popular, with anyone. Dodgeball, burnball, circuit training, or leapfrogging became chores that no one really wanted to do - especially when they were graded as well. As time went on, I lost interest in sports and the joy of exercise dwindled.

In my mid-twenties, however, I felt that something was missing in my everyday life: My body craved exercise, especially because of the long hours at my desk. I knew I had to do something.

My first attempt to just put on my sneakers and run a lap around the block totally went to shit! It was harder than I thought it would be. As a novice runner, I just wasn't used to sticking it out for half an hour at a time. I quickly lost motivation.

Then I decided to become a member of a gym. I hoped to get motivation from other exercisers who, like me, wanted to work on their fitness. But every visit to the gym felt like another school lesson. The equipment was sticky, the air was stuffy, and the noise level was often uncomfortably high. Plus, as a student, I had to dig deep into my pockets to pay for the membership and then to buy the appropriate gym clothes and equipment. All of this seemed exhausting and annoying to me. I felt like I had to force myself to go to the gym. But despite these obstacles, I went. And over time, a positive development set in - I actually became fitter and could do my laps in the park without getting out of breath.

Over time, I switched from running in the gym to the streets and ran outside more and more often. At some point, the weather no longer mattered - I ran in every season, pain-free and without shortness of breath.

Running in nature awakened a whole new passion in me. It gave me a sense of freedom that I had never found in the gym. Each running session was a time out just for me, a moment of peace and reflection. The routes I ran became my personal oases of relaxation. Nature offered me the perfect environment to clear my head, sort out my thoughts and come up with new ideas. And incidentally, running was a great way to relieve stress and keep my body healthy. I felt alive and full of energy.

The love for running grew and I started to deepen my passion. After graduating, I even decided to work in a sports store and train as a running coach. I offered courses in meditative running and began to share my experiences and insights in books. Running became a philosophy of life for me.

Today, running gives me not only physical fitness, but also mental strength. It helps me to know myself better and to overcome my limitations. I have learned that running is much more than physical exercise. It is a source of inner balance and clarity that connects me to myself and the world around me.

I run because it's good for me. It's my way of relieving stress, clearing my head and relaxing. Moving in nature makes me notice and appreciate the beauty of the world around me. While running I have seen the most breathtaking sunsets, discovered new paths and experienced intense moments of joy and happiness. Sometimes while running you find simple solutions to seemingly unsolvable problems. There are moments when you just run without feeling the effort. Among runners, this is known as the "flow state." It is a state where time seems to stand still, where you are in harmony with yourself and nature. It is a moment of absolute unity and pure happiness.

And running is, of course, a vacation in sneakers for me. Every hour I spend doing it is an instant rest for body and mind. If you will, running has taught me that I don't need a vacation far away to be happy and fulfilled. The world is literally my oyster and it is beautiful. I'm grateful that running allows me to experience that beauty in every moment and not have to travel to the other side of the world first.

But running has brought me another important realization: the health of my body is the most valuable asset I own. Our body is our home - we live in it all our lives. Therefore, we should treat it with love and care. We wash our car, take care of our home, but we often forget how important it is to take care of our body. The health of our body affects our well-being, energy and quality of life. That's why it's important that we make time for exercise and sports to strengthen and protect our bodies. Because only a healthy body allows us to live a full and happy life.

Running has shown me that it is not just a sport, but a way of life. It has helped me find my way, connect with myself and enjoy life in all its facets. And I am grateful that I have found this path and can continue to follow it with my running shoes - always with the feeling of freedom and vacation in my heart.

# Discover the world with children's eyes

As a kid, I loved running around on playgrounds: Climbing, sliding, swinging, and trampolining were a perfect after-school afternoon. But it's not just children who need exercise. I'm a firm believer that adults should get some regular exercise, too. And why shouldn't they? Why should this need have changed over the years?

In today's society, it may seem strange for adults to swing or climb, but why really? Some may look at us confused and think of amusement parks or bouldering gyms, but exercise and play are much more than commercial offerings. We shouldn't depend on entrance fees and organized recreational activities. There are so many ways to exercise and have fun without having to pay.

Why not walk barefoot across a meadow or splash in a lake? How about a wild tent sleepover in nature or a round of rollerblading on a quiet trail? There are countless creative and inexpensive ways to be a bit of a kid again and discover the joy of movement.

The evening hours are especially suitable for small adventures. A spontaneous trip to a playground can take us back to our childhood. In some cities there are even special active playgrounds for adults, so-called hot spots. But actually, it's enough to go to any playground nearby. In the evening, these are usually free of children and you have the whole place to yourself. Running barefoot through the sand, swinging on the high bar or swinging can thus become a wonderful way to playfully integrate movement into everyday life and at the same time give space to inner childhood memories.

Such small adventures can not only promote physical activity, but also refresh the soul. They remind us that life doesn't always have to be serious and rigorous, but that it's important to let go every now and then and enjoy life to the fullest. In this way, we can bring back into our lives the lightness and carefree spirit we felt as children.

So why not just go to the playground and have fun? It's a wonderful way to combine exercise, joy and memories. Who would have thought that swinging or climbing on a jungle gym could still be so refreshing and invigorating in adulthood? So let's not be limited by societal norms and expectations, but follow our inner joy and treat ourselves to a little play and fun every now and then - because the child in us will thank us!

# Gold, Silver, Bronze

During my studies, I had the opportunity to attend a lecture on Richard Wagner's four-part opera cycle "Der Ring des Nibelungen." In this 16-hour epic stage festival, Wagner interweaves medieval sagas with Norse myths. The opera consists of four parts and begins with the ugly dwarf Alberich stealing the Rhine gold from the Rhine. From the gold he forges a ring that gives him the power to rule over everything. Wotan, the father of the gods, learns of this and steals the ring from Alberich, who is henceforth cursed. Thus the story of the golden ring takes its course.

Of course, I do not want to recount the plot in detail now, but only refer to my own observations of nature: Gold is indeed in the river. Anyone who walks along the Rhine, the Neckar or any other river on a sunny day knows where the idea for this legend came from. On a sunny day, the water glitters so intensely that one could think that gold lies in it. Here on our Neckar, Alberich does not seem to have stolen the precious metal yet. All the more you can enjoy it when the sun is shining. You can stand on the bridge, for example, or go to the bank, depending on where the sun is at the moment, and admire the natural spectacle. There is something magical about it! But not only the water holds a golden treasure. In autumn, it is the golden leaves in the forests and on the streets.

And something else happens in the warm months: As the sun slowly approaches the horizon in the evening, the light illuminating the trees and leaves turns a warm bronze hue. The intense colors are of breathtaking beauty.

In the early morning hours, when the sky is cloudy and the sun is not yet visible, the landscape appears silvery. On such days, when the wind blows gently and the air is dry, this shimmering color also shows in the river. Gently it glides back and forth with the waves of the water, a beautiful dance with a meditative and slightly melancholic effect. This sight is particularly impressive when there is also fog to be seen. Undoubtedly, this sight has inspired great poets such as Hölderlin, Brentano, Heine, Goethe and Eichendorff to put down on paper their masterpieces about Heidelberg.

Surely there are many other places where color comes into play. Viewed soberly, they are just light effects that can be discovered all over the world, but also right on our doorstep. You don't have to go far afield to experience them. The treasures sparkle before our eyes.

# Was a great time - that can be again

I sit in my worn jeans on the sidewalk and strap the colorful inline skates to my feet. My hair is tied up in a bun and I'm about to set off - I'm looking forward to the upcoming tour. My best friend arrives on her bike, her braided pigtails bobbing back and forth. She tells me about a new jeweler who now does pierced ears. Again, I hang onto the back of her rack and feel the breeze in my face. Together we make our way to the city center, seven kilometers away.

On the way, we stop to fill our water bottles with fresh spring water - a ritual we practice on every tour. Downtown, I stow my skates in my backpack and we take a little stroll. We eat fries and browse for CDs in the music store. We buy a few postcards and pack the festival magazines on display into the backpack.

In between we have to go to a phone booth to let home know that we will be late for dinner tonight. At the art museum we discover an open-air cinema. For only two euros we are in. We don't know what to expect, it's late and tomorrow we have to go back to school. But it doesn't matter what we see or when we get back home. Only the moment counts.

Today it was 20 years ago. But it seems like it was yesterday. I can still remember how much I enjoyed going out on my inline skates, meeting up with my friends after school, going out on the town together and just having a great time. Music also always played a big role and the lyrics of the band JULI still ring in my ears.

This time is not over yet! With Holistay we don't have to mourn our youth and think about the beautiful, carefree life. If we take a vacation at home more often, we get closer to that feeling of life again. We have much more time and we can also rediscover old hobbies, such as inline skating. Since when do we take life so seriously? Let's enjoy the moment again and celebrate life!

# Culinary expedition

# The early bird... goes to market

I'm a late riser and late sleeper by nature, an "owl" as they say. I don't usually get really active until the afternoon and go to bed a little later accordingly. In the morning, I need a little longer to get going. But sometimes I'm overcome by an alertness that gets me out of bed as early as five in the morning. Then I'm in top form and full of energy. Strangely enough, these phases occur mainly at weekends and on vacation, always when I allow myself to sleep in. But that doesn't bother me. In fact, there's something wonderful about it! Because then time feels different. The routine is broken and intensified. I think it's also because everything around me is still very quiet and peaceful. I also move more quietly and slowly, almost in slow motion, and consciously perceive my surroundings. Everything is still asleep and yet the day is dawning.

On days like this, I calmly treat myself to a coffee, which I froth up with almond milk and a little coconut fat, listen to my songbird, and then pack my backpack for a short trip to the market. Here the scenery changes abruptly: Especially in the morning from seven o'clock there is a lot of hustle and bustle. While the sun is still fighting the fog, the merchants are preparing their wares, putting up signs, making coffee, and shouting the latest gossip to each other. The smell of baked bread, pickled olives, herbs and sausages fills the air. Meat sizzles in snack carts, there are curry specialties, burger variations, vegan or even halal dishes - depending on what's on offer. So-called delicacies such as quail eggs, roast venison, special goat cheese, regional honey or grilled grasshoppers can be found at markets like this one. It's incredibly fun to discover and maybe even taste all the delicacies. Sometimes I put together my second breakfast there: A boiled egg here, some cherry tomatoes there, maybe a piece of mountain cheese, and finish with a cup of coffee. Afterwards, I look for a comfortable bench nearby from which I can continue to observe the hustle and bustle. Maybe I'll take a little flower or a few herbs with me for the way back, depending on what appeals to me at the moment.

# I'll be in Asia for a moment

I have been fascinated by Southeast Asia at least since my stay abroad during my studies in Singapore. I am enthusiastic about Asian philosophy. Medicine, cuisine and culture also exert a special attraction on me. Many things are inextricably linked. Tradition and spirituality often flow into modern views and make them so unique. That's why I'm always happy when I pass an Asian store (there are a few in Heidelberg). There I buy my nori leaves (seaweed), hummus, ghee (clarified butter) and sometimes ginseng, fresh mint leaves, ginger and tea.

As soon as I enter the store, I find myself mentally on the other side of the world. Waving cats, ornate fans and Buddha figurines decorate the store. On the shelves are bowls, wok pans, rice stoves, chopsticks, tiger balm and tea sets. I love walking slowly through the store, browsing the shelves and engaging with the products. I don't know most of it and it's fun to keep trying something new and going on a journey of discovery. Sometimes I get a fortune cookie as a gift at the checkout - that's not only super nice, but also somehow typically Asian. Whenever I get wanderlust for Southeast Asia, I visit an Asian store like this.

# Eating fit and healthy

I have always enjoyed going on culinary expeditions locally and trying local restaurants from all over the world. You can do that especially well in Heidelberg and the surrounding area! There is hardly anything that I haven't tried yet. I love the tasty and aromatic Spanish cuisine, the spicy Indian dishes, the exotic African dishes, the spicy Korean dishes, the sweet and sour Chinese creations and the hearty Eastern European dishes.

Over the course of time, especially since I have become professionally involved with the topic of health and nutrition, I also consciously pay attention to healthy and natural foods when eating out. I sometimes leave out sauces, dips and dressings, choose baked instead of deep-fried dishes and always prefer fresh food to pickled versions.

Healthy eating and vacations have a lot in common! Eating healthy on vacation is important because it directly affects our well-being and energy. It provides us with the nutrients we need to feel fit and vital. A balanced diet strengthens our immune system and helps prevent fatigue, mood swings and digestive problems.

Of course, you're allowed to make an exception and treat yourself to a bag of chips, a cold cola or an ice cream. But healthy eating does not mean giving up pleasure and taste. On the contrary, on vacation we can discover and enjoy the variety of flavors of the local cuisine. If you go out for a delicious meal, you won't even think about pizza, French fries or gummy bears. How about a delicious quinoa burger, a colorful Buddha Bowl or deep-fried zoodles? For dessert, go for sweet chia pudding, spicy golden milk or frothy matcha tea.

Opting for healthy options will pamper your palate and boost your health at the same time. A healthy diet on permanent vacation - and that's what Holistay essentially is - allows us to experience the beautiful life permanently full of energy, well-being and joy and to make the most of our time.

# Literary expedition

# The world in books

My love of books allows me to travel literarily to the most beautiful places in the world without physically setting out. With the help of literature, I discover new worlds from the comfort of my sofa. Travelogues with vivid descriptions of landscapes, cultures, people, and encounters put me in the situation as if I were actually there. My imagination is stimulated and I can embark on a journey that tangibly transports me to these faraway places. The magic of books enables me to discover the beauty and diversity of our world and to be enchanted by words wherever I go.

What travel promises can also be experienced from books: By reading about the daily life, food habits, festivals and history of a place, we expand our knowledge of different cultures, customs and traditions. This allows us to broaden our perspective on the diversity of our world and gain deeper insight into global communities. There are other benefits as well: Those who discover new places in books become curious, immerse themselves in the stories and adventures of others, forget the world around them, recharge their batteries and quench their wanderlust. Last but not least, travel stories broaden our horizons. By engaging with other points of view and ways of life, we broaden our view of the world and deepen our understanding of other cultures and people.

In the following I would like to introduce - sorted by country - some writing globetrotters with whom I have already undertaken interesting journeys of thought. Of course, I can't cover all the countries of the world (unfortunately, I haven't read that many books yet), but the journey has just begun. In my mind, I'm already packing my bags and I'm excited to see where it goes next. Until then, we will still travel some beautiful corners of the world:

# Across Germany

**Hysterie des Körpers. Der Lauf meines Lebens** („Hysteria of the Body. The course of my life") German Edition by Joey Kelly (2011)

The book tells the story of Joey, member of the famous Kelly Family and passionate athlete. His outstanding achievements in endurance and extreme sports have made him internationally famous alongside his career as a singer. So he considers running a marathon merely as warm-up training for his participation in Ultraman competitions all over the world. One day Joey makes the courageous decision to cross Germany on foot, alone and without any money in his pocket. The adventure begins at the North Sea and ends at the summit of the Zugspitze, Germany's highest mountain. Along the way, Joey looks back on his time as a member of the Kelly Family and recounts breathtaking experiences in the desert, at the North Pole and in the mountains. The reader learns how Joey got into extreme sports, how he slept, washed and ate on his trek through Germany.

If you are interested in Joey Kelly's story, you can also read his new book No Limits: 7 Continents. 100,000 Kilometers. 100 Challenges. Here, the extreme athlete tells of all his previous travel experiences from the Sahara to Siberia to the South Pole. The book is available in German and English and has been on sale since 2023.

# France

### The Monks and Me: How 40 Days at Thich Nhat Hanh's French Monastery Guided Me Home by Mary Paterson (2012)

Mary, a young woman from Canada, has recently experienced bereavement. During this difficult time, she decides to spend some time in Plum Village, a monastery in the south of France founded and inhabited by the famous Buddhist monk Thich Nath Hanh (†2022). Her retreat lasts 40 days, during which she not only comes to rest, but also meets interesting people and shares her observations, experiences and insights in 40 small chapters. For anyone interested in monastic life, especially Theravada-style, the book offers fascinating insights. On the very first day, Mary experiences a situation that makes it clear that some comforts we take for granted do not exist in the monastery. What happens when you are just soaped up in the shower and the water suddenly stops flowing? At that moment, Mary begins her first Buddhist practice.

**Camus: Das Ideal der Einfachheit. Eine Biografie**
("Camus: The Ideal of Simplicity. A Biography") German
Edition by Iris Radisch (2014)

This biography is dedicated to the life of the French writer,
philosopher and Nobel Prize winner Albert Camus. His story is
closely linked to his two homelands, Algeria and later France. The
North African country of Algeria, where Camus was born and
grew up, was an important colony of France until its
independence in 1962. In this impressive work, author Radisch
describes in detail the way of life and the special features of the
two countries, which she presents in stark contrast to each other:
On the one hand, the sunny country with its beaches and the
simplicity of everyday life; on the other, the grey, rainy and highly
complex metropolis of Paris, to which Camus moved due to the
circumstances of the war and where he wrote his masterpieces.
He remains true to his search for the absurdity of life. Algeria and
France play an important role again and again.

# Spain

**I'm Off Then: Losing and Finding Myself on the Camino
de Santiago** by Hape Kerkeling (2009)

Although there are already numerous film adaptations and other
works with similar titles, this book is a valuable treasure in the
world of walking literature. Although it is set on a path of inner

contemplation, tranquillity and spirituality, Hape Kerkeling always manages to make us laugh in good company. He encounters warm-hearted, but also bizarre and pitiable personalities. The book even has the ability to put the reader in a trance-like state and provide exciting borderline experiences. It is fun to share in Kerkeling's experiences and accompany him a bit on his way to Santiago de Compostela.

**The Idle Traveller. The Art Of Slow Travel** by Dan Kieran (2013)

The adventure begins right on your doorstep, and that is not an empty promise, but an enjoyable fact, as Dan Kieran tells us in this book. Suffering from a fear of flying, his journey begins slowly. Instead of taking a three-hour flight from England to Poland for his friend's wedding, he opts for a two-day train journey across Europe, which turns out to be a wonderful experience. He finds time for literature, for reflection and meets interesting people whose stories he writes down. The life stories touch him deeply and make him think. Dan finds that travelling slowly leads to thoughts and insights that one would never gain on a short flight. Inspired by this experience, the Brit plans further journeys, which he undertakes on foot, by train or even in a milk float. He observes nature closely, listens attentively to conversations and sees his surroundings in a new way that invites you to dream, linger and imitate.

# Russia

**Verliebt in Sankt Petersburg. Meine russische Reise**
(„In love with Saint Petersburg. My Russian Journey") German
Edition by Lena Gorelik (2008)

The main character of this book is a woman born in St.
Petersburg who, as a so-called contingent refugee, had to leave
Germany at the age of one because of the Russian-Jewish
conflicts. Now she returns, not only as a curious explorer, but also
as a journalist and writer. Her goal is to get to know better the
country she once had to leave. In Saint Petersburg, she
experiences a very personal encounter that enables her to
understand Russia beyond clichés and superficial stereotypes.
The journey connects her more deeply with her homeland and
she discovers the many facets of the country that has far more to
offer than vodka, furs and White Nights. These experiences make
the book a unique journey of discovery that gives the reader an
extraordinary insight into Russia.

**Sovietistan: Travels in Turkmenistan, Kazakhstan,
Tajikistan, Kyrgyzstan, and Uzbekistan** by Erika Faltend
(2021)

A few years ago, the USSR, the Soviet Union, was a powerful
nation founded in 1922 and made up of countries such as Russia,
the Baltic States (Lithuania, Estonia, Latvia), Ukraine, Belarus
and other states that joined -Istan, such as Turkmenistan,

Kazakhstan, Tajikistan, Kyrgyzstan and Uzbekistan. After its dissolution in 1991, however, the region's diversity and continuing rift between dictatorship, violence and corruption became apparent. Out of curiosity, Norwegian journalist Erika Faltend set out on a journey through these very different countries. In her book, she gives us a fascinating insight into a region that often seems distant and sometimes dangerous, but holds incredible treasures and stories that leave us amazed.

**Mut für zwei: Mit der Transsibirischen Eisenbahn in unsere neue Welt** („Courage for Two: With the Trans-Siberian Railway to Our New World") by Julia Malchow (2017)

In this travelogue, tourist Julia Malchow takes us on an extraordinary journey through Russia and Mongolia - an unforgettable trip on the famous Trans-Siberian Railway. But she does not travel alone, for Julia is accompanied by her three-year-old son, who plays a decisive role in her stories. Sincerely and stirringly, Julia tells of the encounters and adventures she experiences on the train. On the long train journey, damp cloths, biscuits and tea from the constantly boiling samovar become precious companions. The train journey becomes an experience in which the small, everyday things suddenly take on great significance. Particularly impressive is the role of her three-year-old son as a "mediator" between the cultures. Although Julia herself does not speak a word of Russian, she succeeds in communicating with her fellow passengers through her child. Because children don't need language. Her son proves to be a bridge builder and mediates between people of different countries and cultures in his very own way. Even though the train journey has its pitfalls, it becomes a wonderful and moving journey between West and East. Julia's honest narratives allow the reader to share first-hand her experiences and feelings during the trip and she proves that great adventures are possible even with small children. The author shows that a trip with a three-year-old son is not only feasible, but can also be a source of joy and learning.

# South East Asia

### Married to Bhutan: How One Woman Got Lost, Said 'I Do,' and Found Bliss by Linda Leaming (2011)

Bhutan, a small country in the Himalayas between India and Nepal, is considered difficult to access and thus isolated from the rest of the world. The living conditions of most people in Bhutan appear very simple by our standards: there is a lack of electricity, running water and decent roads. Nevertheless, the Bhutanese are considered the happiest people in the world. This may be because they are self-sufficient and maintain a close connection with nature and their fellow human beings. Buddhism is the state religion and the well-being of the population has top priority. Thus, the education and health care system is free for Bhutanese. However, different rules apply to tourists and immigrants. To avoid mass tourism, the infrastructure has not been further developed. In addition, there are strict entry regulations with high fees and strict controls. Those who nevertheless muster the courage and take on the strain of working and living here - be it through a scholarship, an exchange program or even marriage - will get to know a new world. So did Linda Leasing, an American who was so electrified after a vacation in Bhutan that she only wanted to find a way back. She started as an English teacher and immersed herself once again in everyday life in Bhutan.

**Mammon Inc.** by Hwee Hwee Tan (2001)

Most people only know Singapore as a stopover on their way to Indonesia, Australia, the Philippines or New Zealand. Unfortunately, few take the time to really get to know Singapore. What many do not know: Behind the glittering facade of Asia's wealthiest metropolis with its skyscrapers, casinos and air-conditioned shopping malls lies a fascinating cultural mix based on an interesting history and rich traditions.

In her novel, author Hwee Tan tells of the discrepancy between the aspiring, successful and money-oriented life and the simple but fulfilling and quiet everyday life of a research assistant at the university. Again and again, the protagonist is faced with decisions: Should she pursue her passion for the humanities, which will probably never earn her much money, or should she accept the enticing offer of an internationally successful and expanding company? Through this narrative, the reader not only gets to know Singapore, but also dives deep into a way of thinking that is not so dissimilar to ours.

**Zanskar und ein Leben mehr** („Zanskar and one life more")
German Edition by Ulli Olvedi (2015)

The book tells the story of a young woman whose mother is from
Tibet and father from Switzerland. She feels the need to explore
her roots. But not only that - above all she is in search of her
missing mother. She went to Nepal to live for some time in a
Buddhist monastery and left only her diaries. There is no trace of
her. So the daughter also travels to Nepal, takes the diaries and
learns more about her mother, with whom she never really had a
good relationship. The books and the stories in them change
everything. They also question the young protagonist's own
concept of life, her attitude to family, career and partnership. The
diaries give insight into the everyday life of a Buddhist woman in
Nepal. Overall, they convey images of an unknown country high
in the Himalayan mountains. How does it live so secluded in an
old Buddhist monastery? These questions are answered in the
book.

**Child of the Jungle: The True Story of a Girl Caught
Between Two Worlds** by Sabine Kuegler (2007)

The story is an autobiographical account by Sabine of her
childhood and youth in the deep jungles of West Papua,
Indonesia. As the daughter of German missionaries, Sabine is
sent with her family to the remote region of the Fayu tribes to
convert them to Christianity. The family must face the challenges
of jungle life, with dangerous animals, unpredictable weather

conditions, and the cultural divide between their German heritage and the native Fayu. The girl quickly develops a deep connection with nature and the Fayu. She learns their language, immerses herself in their customs and forms close friendships with the local children. As Sabine gets older, her interest in the modern world outside the jungle grows and she feels the inner conflict between her love for the Fayu and her longing for her German roots. Finally, the family decides to leave the jungle and return to Germany. For the young woman, it is one of the most difficult decisions of her life. She tells about it in this book.

# East Asia

**Kim und Struppi. Ferien in Nordkorea** („Kim and Snowy: Vacation in North Korea") German Edition by Christian Eisert (2015)

Most people will not plan a vacation to North Korea on their own. We leave that to others like the satirist Christian Eisert, who tells us in an entertaining way about his experiences in this country. Reading this book is a special pleasure because Eisert uses his talent (humor). North Korea lives in a restrictive dictatorship. Since 1948, the country has been separated from the South, with which it maintains a bitter enmity. Missile and nuclear weapons have always been among its flagship programs. Although the great man Kim Il Sung has been dead for nearly 30 years, he is still officially president. He is hailed as the "creator" of the North Korean landscape. His literary talent is particularly admirable: he claims to be the only writer who has managed to write a book every day. Kim Jong-il, also known as "the madman with the bomb," died of heart failure in 2011 but continues to be present as the "eternal general secretary. Today, his son Kim Jong-Un, born in 1984, is the country's supreme leader. He attended school in Switzerland under a false identity as the alleged son of a North Korean ambassador. He was not only shy and a basketball fan, but also a diligent and ambitious student.

Now Christian Eisert travels to a country that tries to maintain a façade behind which oppression, labor camps and famine are hidden. Again and again he looks behind the scenes. Will he ever be allowed to re-enter the country after the book has been on the bestseller list for a long time? It certainly hasn't escaped the notice of "Rocket Man Kim," as former U.S. President Trump affectionately calls him.

**Schlaflos in Seoul. Korea für ein Jahr** („Sleepless in Seoul: Korea for a year") German Edition by Vera Hohleiter (2009)

Most of us don't know much more about South Korea than that the country is in constant conflict with its northern neighbor. In this country, we may be familiar with Korean cuisine or buy electronics from Korean manufacturers such as Samsung or LG. The car brands Hyundai or Daewoo, which are produced in Korea, are also well-known. Occasionally, K-pop (Korean pop music) also spills over to us. Gangnam Style, for example, has conquered our dance floors for a while. The book "Sleepless in

Korea" tells the story of Vera, a young woman who decides to live in Seoul for a while. South Korea is a fascinating, but for us very foreign country and curiosity drives her to get to know this unknown country better. During her stay in Seoul, she also meets her future husband, whom she gets to know at a job outside the turbulent megacity. In an entertaining way, she tells of her personal experiences in everyday life, whether at language school, at work or in exchanges with Korean friends.

**Meine Suche nach dem Nichts: Wie ich tausend Kilometer auf dem japanischen Jakobsweg lief und was ich dabei fand** („My Search for Nothing: How I Walked a Thousand Miles on the Japanese Way of St. James and What I Found Along the Way") German Edition by Lena Schabl (2019)

After a long illness (Epstein-Barr virus), Lena Schnabl, a Japanologist and journalist living in Berlin, decides to walk the Japanese Way of St. James on the island of Shikoku, one of the oldest paths in the world. She covers 1,300 kilometers on foot and visits 88 Buddhist temples along the way. She meets other pilgrims, falls in love and also consciously chooses solitude. For she is looking for nothingness and experiences happiness, which she packs into this book in a witty and sympathetic way. Along the way, one learns a lot about Japanese culture, its peculiarities and beauties, and admires that she, as a young woman in poor health, gets through all this alone.

# Australia

**Mutant Message Down Under: A Woman's Journey into Dreamtime Australia** by Marlo Morgan (1994)

There are many ways to travel a country and get to know its culture, people, language, traditions and customs. Most people associate Australia with the classic image of the backpacker who seeks the great adventure Down Under for a year after graduating from school. With his 50-liter backpack, he stands on the side of the road with his thumb out, waiting for a ride. Perhaps he'll see kangaroos (or be served them as a delicacy), snorkel and encounter crocodiles. He will also encounter the world's oldest culture - the Aborigines, who today are often unemployed, poorly integrated and socially disadvantaged.

But there is also another approach to this land that the American doctor chooses. Her true story is published as a novel in order to protect the people (a certain tribe of Aborigines) it is about. The doctor has been working for several years with so-called "mixed Aborigines" in the city who are suicidal. Through her research, the doctor gains international attention and is personally invited by an Australian Aboriginal tribe. Not knowing what to expect, she accepts the invitation and sets out. For three months, as the "chosen one", she is to get to know real life in the bush. In the process, she learns about the life of the people who have inhabited Australia for 50,000 years. They possess ancient knowledge and an extraordinary way of dealing with nature, which the doctor learns about and which will have a lasting impact on her life.

## South and North America

**Abenteuer Urwald. Ausgesetzt ohne Ausrüstung. Die Morde um Tatunca Nara** („Adventure jungle. Exposed without equipment. The murders around Tatunca Nara") German Edition by Rüdiger Nehberg (2005)

Anyone involved in survival, bushcraft, prepping, outdoor or adventure vacations is also familiar with the stories of survival artist Rüdiger Nehberg (†2020), also known as Sir Vival. The former baker from Germany is known for making his way through the jungle without equipment or preparation or crossing the Pacific Ocean on a homemade raft. But he is also known for his humanitarian commitment to the jungle Indians, the rainforest and the fight against female genital mutilation in Africa.

In his book "Adventure Jungle," his story begins with him abandoning himself somewhere in the Amazon and finding his way back to civilization. He sleeps in his self-knotted hammock, fights hunger, gets injured and faces the challenges of the caimans. He also tells the story of Tatunca, the false chief of the forest.

Tatunca, as Nehberg discovered during his research, is actually from Nuremberg and has had a difficult childhood. Under a false identity, he goes into the jungle and poses there as the chief of an allegedly secret Indian tribe to which only he has access. Curious journalists or skeptics who make contact with him disappear from the scene over time. Nehberg follows their story and makes interesting discoveries.

## Epic Survival: Extreme Adventure, Stone Age Wisdom, and Lessons in Living From a Modern Hunter-Gatherer
by Matt Graham (2015)

Author and survival expert Matt Graham is probably the best person to give us an insight into the lives of our ancestors, the hunter-gatherers. How did they go about their daily lives? How did they make hunting weapons, how did they sleep, how did they seek shelter, how did they generate heat, and how did they survive the cold winter months?

Even as a child and teenager, the young American was interested in a way of life that was close to nature and self-sufficient. He began sleeping outside more and more often, taking cold showers, eating mainly natural foods, walking and making his own clothes. Along the way, he helped out on a reservation to be even closer to nature. In this way, he quickly developed what he calls "primitive skills," which he now shares as a survival expert on tours and television shows. He has crossed America on foot several times, including on the famous Pacific Crest Trail, and reports in detail on his experiences in his book. In doing so, he emphasizes that it's not just physical strength that counts, but mental strength above all. His experiences in the wilderness are impressive.

Nevertheless, he is drawn back to civilization again and again, whether out of loneliness, in search of a partner, or because of bureaucratic obligations. But the longing for the wilderness remains and drives him back again and again.

**Into the Wild** by Jon Krakauer (1996)

The book tells the story of Chris McCandless, a young man who escapes modern life in search of the true, authentic life. His search, however, ends tragically in the loneliness of Alaska and finally in his early death. Thanks to the numerous records he left behind, his short but impressive life can be reconstructed. The film tells the story of a young achiever and college graduate from a wealthy Washington home who takes a very different path than expected. The focus is on the tensions between father and son. Chris can no longer withstand the pressure to perform and longs to break free.

Secretly, he finally leaves his orderly life, gives away all his belongings, burns his car and initially travels across the country. He roams through forests, works on plantations, gets himself a canoe and finally makes it to Alaska, where he finds shelter in an old, discarded school bus - until winter sets in and puts an early end to his adventure.

**Reise durch einen einsamen Kontinent. Unterwegs in Kolumbien, Ecuador, Peru, Bolivien und Chile** („Journey through a lonely continent. On the road in Colombia, Ecuador, Peru, Bolivia and Chile") German Edition by Andreas Altmann (2017)

The book begins with an impressive opening. The travel reporter, already known from many other books (such as "Meet Buddha, Kill Him" or "Instruction Manual for the World"), is known for not mincing words. He rails against the church, loves women, enjoys life and is a keen observer. From the very first lines, he warns the reader, "This book is not about hotel recommendations, sightseeing or colorful folklore, but about encounters on the street with real life - unadulterated, brutal, often stenchy and, above all, lonely." Nevertheless, his encounters with people are marked by great depth and empathy.

The travel reporter crosses the country by bus. He is annoyed by the constant sound of television and remembers the time when passengers still talked and laughed with each other instead of watching violent scenes on TV for hours. He visits places marked by misunderstood poets, experiences a soccer game with blind players, visits a young German woman in prison, and ventures into mines where he meets people who only "warm" themselves with alcohol and cheap relationships.

The book captivates the reader from the very beginning. With every sentence, one dives deeper into a continent that is both frightening and fascinating. A book that you can no longer put down.

## Around the world (and to yourself)

**Das Ende ist mein Anfang. Ein Vater, ein Sohn und die große Reise des Lebens** („The end is my beginning. A Father, a Son and the Great Journey of Life") German Edition by Tiziano Terzani (2017)

The story of Tiziano Terzani, reporter, cultural mediator and correspondent, who is confronted with his cancer. He tries to trust both Western doctors and alternative healing methods, but in the end his fate is inevitable. In this book he tells impressively and authentically about his farewell.

Although it is about the disease, the affirmation of life is always in the foreground. Tiziano was a cosmopolitan who led an eventful life and was at home everywhere in the world. This is impressively described in the conversations with his son.

The book is about the search for the meaning of life, about the search for oneself and finally about unconditional letting go. After reading it, one sees the world with different eyes. It is a kind of book of life that invites you to pause and take a moving journey to what makes us human.

**Das große Los. Wie ich bei Günther Jauch eine halbe Million gewann und einfach losfuhr** („The big draw: How I won half a million on Günther Jauch and just drove off") German Edition by Meike Winnemuth (2013)

Meike Winnemuth, a funny, likeable and quick-witted woman, wins "Who Wants to be a Millionaire" and then decides to go on a world tour. On her journey through cities like Sydney, Mumbai, San Francisco and Copenhagen, she gradually realizes that she didn't need all that money to live the life she had always dreamed of. This realization can also be applied to her own life. What happens when you really allow yourself to do anything? How does it feel to live the life that others only dream of? And what does it take to lead a fulfilled and happy life? Meike Winnemuth shows that you don't need a lot of money to answer these questions for yourself. After her trip around the world, she now lives minimalistically in a small apartment and has a small dog by her side.

In her follow-up book "To make a long story short: On the Outrageous Happiness of Being in the World," she sums it up once again: it doesn't take much to be happy. Everyday problems can be quickly overcome and joie de vivre can be found in the most banal situations. It challenges ingrained thought patterns and stimulates reflection. With these two books, Meike Winnemuth definitely brings more sunshine into everyday life and on the journey home.

**Eat Pray Love: One Woman's Search for Everything** by Elizabeth Gilbert (2007)

A classic (not only for women) and a must for all travel lovers: A dissatisfied woman full of wanderlust, romantic longing, curiosity and in search of love, happiness and spirituality decides, shortly after her life has come apart at the seams, to set off into the wide world.

Her first stop is Italy, where she rediscovers the joy and beauty of life. She celebrates the beauty of the language and the pleasures of Italian cuisine. Then her path takes her to India, where she finds inner peace, contemplation and balance. Here she also learns the art of abstinence and has deep conversations with her new friends. Finally, she answers the call to Indonesia, a country she has visited before, to study with an old master, make new friends, and love life. There she finally meets, at first uncertainly and hesitantly, the love of her life. In the end, of course, there is a happy ending! A successful masterpiece that, quite incidentally, makes you think and awakens your admiration for the little things in life. A book that you take firmly into your heart after reading it.

**Hector and the Search for Happiness** by Francois Lelord (2010)

French psychoanalyst Hector is known for his humorous stories and his chronically dissatisfied patients, whom he finally wants to really help. His book is about the search for happiness, and

Hector finds that he simply can't stand the constant whining anymore. Why are people so dissatisfied and sad, even though they are actually doing well? Hector finally wants to get to the bottom of this question and embarks on a long trip around the world to learn from other people and cultures. How do others deal with their problems? What makes them happy and what can we learn from them? With each lesson he learns, Hector establishes a set of rules for a happy and content life. Those who follow these rules actually have no more reason to complain. But unfortunately, in everyday life we often quickly forget the lessons we have learned. All the more reason to pick up this wonderfully amusing book and join Hector on his quest for happiness.

**Loslassen. Wie ich die Welt entdeckte und verzichten lernte** („Letting go. How I discovered the world and learned to do without") German Edition by Katharina Finke (2017)

More than seven years ago, Katharina decided to give up her apartment, travel the world and work on the road - everything she needed fit into two suitcases. And that's what this book is about. After the end of her relationship, she and her ex-boyfriend break up their shared apartment in Hamburg. He takes most of the furniture with him, while she decides to part with the rest of the things and sell them. She feels that these items would only disturb her on her travels. Katharina is from northern Germany, studied tourism in Heidelberg and works mainly as a correspondent, copywriter and journalist. She travels to different countries like Portugal, England, USA, India, New Zealand and

China and stays either on a temporary basis or directly with friends. Over time, she makes many friends and becomes very interested in the lives of the people around her. Although she always returns to Berlin, she is always drawn to the wider world. During her travels, she becomes more and more thoughtful and self-critical. She is aware that traveling so much is not environmentally friendly, but she had to go through this experience to come to this realization. One accompanies her on her air travels, jogs with her in her mind through Central Park, grieves, discovers, questions and falls in love anew. Her experiences make you think about your own life and the environment.

In the meantime, there is a continuation of her story, in which she tells about her new life "in a threesome". Because, Katharina becomes a mother and now finds herself in an interesting situation. How does it feel to be a minimalist who only travels and actually celebrates all freedoms? Isn't family life a contradiction in terms, or does she manage to reconcile both? She tells us this in her new book entitled "Go life. The courage to let go and discover the world as a family" (2021).

**Zwei nach Shanghai: 13600 Kilometer mit dem Fahrrad von Deutschland nach China** („Two to Shanghai: 13600 kilometres by bike from Germany to China") German Edition by Hansen und Paul Hoepner (2015)

The book is based on the 2012 television documentary about the seven-month bicycle tour of the Hansen brothers and Paul, which was financed through crowdfunding. The two brothers are trained designers specializing in photography, product and web design and had a shared dream of cycling around the world. In this book, they take the reader with them on their adventure through the East: the twins cycle from Berlin to Shanghai, a distance of 13,600 km. Along the way, they cross countries such as Russia, Kazakhstan, Kyrgyzstan, Tibet and China. They sleep in tents, bathe in rivers and meet friendly people. There is a breathtaking beauty to the landscape shots in the film. But the narration in the book also captures the imagination and you can put yourself right into their adventure: You sweat, pedal, suffer and laugh along in your thoughts. Of course, it's understandable that such a tour and the exertions involved can also lead to serious arguments. But the two brothers always pull themselves together and master the physical and emotional ups and downs of their journey.

A few years later, the brothers wrote about other adventures, including their trip around the world in 80 days (and without any money), and finally their circumnavigation of the globe by boat, now with a small family and a dog on board.

# Slow, Holy and Tiny

Finally, I'd like to share three ways to travel without really going far. Now that we've learned what exciting adventures there are at home and in the immediate vicinity, we can go to places and places that we have less on our radar. But that doesn't mean the journey there is any less adventurous. As I said, it doesn't matter the distance or the mode of transportation. Let's go!

## Excursion? S-l-o-o-o-o-o-w travel

It doesn't always have to be exotic destinations like Hawaii, Bali or South Africa to experience a fulfilling trip. Often it is enough to explore the next place, the next bigger city or a certain region nearby.

For example, I always try to walk to places that are less than 20 kilometres away. Otherwise, I like to take the train or bus and combine the trip with small hikes. That way, I can experience the landscape with all my senses and let the surroundings take effect on me. It's really amazing how beautiful the area is where I live and how often I overlook the beauty around me in everyday life.

The magic word for such discoveries is "Slow".

With this type of travel, you switch off the speed completely. To do this, for example, I take public transportation like the regional train. Yes, it stops in every little town, and that's a good thing. Because then you can consciously concentrate on your surroundings - according to the motto: the journey is the destination. On such slow journeys, I am really on the road with body and soul. I can consciously and extensively deal with my goal or intention while I look out of the moving train at the passing landscape and notice the people getting on and off. There is more time to read and write or just to look out the window. This way of traveling is nothing new or special in itself. Just a few years ago, and even in many countries outside Europe, slow travel was the norm. But precisely because we are often in a hurry in our hectic everyday lives, it does us good to slow down.

---

### Tourism advantages

-   The encounter with foreign cultures, traditions and languages enables intercultural exchange and enriches one's own knowledge and understanding.
-   Contact with locals strengthens the bond with the country and its people, and prejudices can be overcome.
-   Tourism promotes economic growth in developing countries by creating jobs and supporting local businesses.
-   It improves infrastructure such as roads, hotels and restaurants, which also benefits the local population.
-   Tourism offers recreation and relaxation, as it is often easier to switch off from everyday life in foreign surroundings.
-   By visiting sights and cultural events, foreign cultures and traditions are perceived and appreciated.
-   Traveling makes it possible to get to know new perspectives, to educate oneself and to broaden one's own horizons.
-   The tourism sector creates numerous jobs in various fields such as gastronomy, hotel business, transport and entertainment.

- The exchange of people from different countries promotes multiculturalism and contributes to international understanding

## Tourism disadvantages

- Tourism can lead to environmental pollution, destruction of nature and waste problems, especially in heavily frequented tourist areas.
- In countries that rely heavily on tourism, seasonal or financial fluctuations can affect the economy.
- An increase in tourism may also be associated with an increase in prostitution and disease.
- Mass tourism can lead to the destruction of culture and tradition, as the authenticity of certain places and customs can be lost.
- Noise pollution, odor pollution, and water pollution are negative impacts of tourism on the environment and local people.
- The influx of tourists can lead to traffic chaos and crowded places, which in turn can affect the quality of life of local people.
- Tourism can lead to the urbanization of certain areas, which can result in the displacement of local people and the loss of traditional ways of life.
- In some cases, tourism can increase crime and drug trafficking in a region.
- Cultural exchange can lead to alienation from indigenous culture, as tourism demand requires certain changes and adaptations.
- In some countries, tourism can be associated with forced labor and child labor
- The increase in tourism leads to higher $CO_2$ consumption due to transportation and operation of tourist facilities.
- There are cases where tourists disregard local customs and behave disrespectfully towards the culture and habits of the local population

I like to associate being on the road with a certain song. Sometimes I select a specific music album beforehand and download it to my phone. Or I simply let myself be surprised on the road by a song that I pick up here and there. This often happens in cafés or in the middle of the city, when street artists are playing music.

Especially in the summer, I'm often lucky enough to pass by a city festival or open-air festival on my city trips. There are great concerts by great bands and the best part: admission is usually free! There I like to sit down and enjoy the concert. Such spontaneous and unplanned events often become the highlights of my trip.

It doesn't take much to feel completely happy and experience unforgettable moments. Sometimes a balmy summer evening in a beautiful place, in a cozy bar or restaurant, at a lovingly set table with candle or lantern light in the background, accompanied by a gentle breeze and happy people around you, is enough.

And music always has a special effect! Like a photograph, it captures the moment and preserves it forever. If you listen to the song again later, memories are awakened, just like when you leaf through a photo album. Years later, the connection between music and event still works. Memories come alive. Music enriches travel and makes it special.

## Why hurry? Advantages of slowness

- Slowness has nothing to do with inertia or laziness. In fact, it used to be considered a desirable virtue and was interpreted more as serenity. People who are serene have inner peace, are better able to deal with difficult situations and are more satisfied overall. In addition, one can better concentrate on the really important things in life.
- Not everything that is fast is automatically good, even if current social trends like to tell us the opposite (in the sense of "higher, faster, further").
- Slowness often enables a higher quality of things and experiences because you take more time for them. Time creates depth, appreciation, enjoyment and often precision.
- In slowness, one can follow one's individual rhythm much more precisely and thus find oneself better.
- Slowness is an ideal remedy for the hectic pace of everyday life. It reduces stress and helps to concentrate on the essentials again.
- The senses are sharpened again when one moves slowly.
- The environment is perceived more consciously: Smells, sounds and tastes become more intense.
- Those who are slow are in a state of flow and are contemplative, so that nothing can upset them.

# HolyStay – Local Abbey Tours

When I tell friends and acquaintances about my last New Year's Eve trip, that I spent a few days in a Zen monastery to end the year meditatively, the first question that often comes up is which Asian country I was in. Why Asia in particular, I ask in amazement. Because Buddhism has its roots there? Because one associates Zen monasteries with the Far East? Because one automatically thinks that one has to travel to escape from everyday life?

What hardly anyone knows is that my monastery is only a few hours away from my home by train. It is a German monastery with Vietnamese and German nuns and monks. And the real journey begins when everything around you becomes completely still and motionless - in the meditation posture. In the monastery there are common meals in the morning and in the evening. One can also fast, which I certainly considered. Nevertheless, I participated in the common meal with my cup of tea, because it is really extraordinary: During the meal, people do not talk to each other as they usually do, but each of the 80 or so guests concentrates entirely on his or her meal. Mindfulness is the guiding principle.

In the monastery there are several meditation rooms where you can retreat individually and meditate for yourself. But there is also the possibility to meditate in community. In the largest room, there is meditation at 5:30 in the morning and at 7:00 in the evening under the guidance of the religious. In between there is nothing special to do. You can visit the library, take a walk in the garden, warm up in the neighbouring teahouse or join a yoga class. You can also retire to your room at any time to sleep, think or simply do nothing. But that's not so easy. Suddenly you have so much time on your hands!

You get a good introduction at the official ceremony in the evening. This ceremony is actually quite unspectacular, but the bowing before the large golden Buddha statue has of course a religious note. Afterwards, everyone takes a comfortable sitting position on the soft carpet, wraps a wool blanket around their shoulders if necessary, closes their eyes and listens to the Sanskrit chants until the bell rings. Then it becomes completely silent. With the first chime of the bell, the official meditation begins. Breathe in, breathe out. Observe thoughts, let thoughts go. Breathe in, breathe out. Find peace, concentrate. Push questions aside, push ideas aside, let go of memories, focus on breath, ignore pain. Inhale, exhale. Concentrate again, ignore sounds, ignore body sensations. Inhale, exhale. Feel calm, stay in this state. The second chime ends the meditation. Many slowly stand up, bow once more to Buddha, and quietly leave the room. Others remain seated, linger, and are probably already in nirvana.

For several years I have been practicing meditation and immersing myself in nothingness. Sometimes, when everything around me goes completely silent, I enter a state of complete timelessness, numbness and disembodiment. First, I no longer feel my legs. Then I no longer notice the hands that are resting on my legs. Breathing becomes suspiciously slow and barely perceptible. One moment I am asking myself questions or reminding myself to concentrate, and the next moment there is simply nothing. No more questions, no more I-consciousness, everything around me becomes completely unimportant. This state can last a few minutes or even hours. I can't say for sure. It is as if I am asleep, fully conscious. I am there, wide awake, but somehow not. If someone wants to practice by themselves, I recommend meditating in the evening, in a relaxed state and preferably with no time limit - just open into the night. That always works best for me.

The time I spend in such a monastery at the end of the year is incredibly good for me. I drink a lot of tea, sleep (of course!) more than usual, read, write, talk to the other monastery visitors and maybe paint mandalas. I walk a lot. Some days feel like weeks. The days pass slowly. I don't have a mobile phone or laptop with me during this time. Going without solid meals is a bit of a challenge at first. But the body and mind adjust. They work on the back burner, gather strength, process the past months, let go, conclude. I don't have to actively do anything, it just happens. I watch, don't interfere, don't discuss, don't argue. I just let go.

Whether ashrams, Zen or Benedictine monasteries - they are all places of self-encounter, relaxation and silence. You don't have to go far away for this, but often find this experience within yourself. A wonderful place to make the next home vacation a Holy-Stay.

# Alternative accommodation

And now a dwelling that measures only two to four square meters: the tent!

Weighing only one to three kilograms, this shelter is light, compact and handy. Together with the sleeping bag and some other utensils, it fits easily into the backpack. That's all you need. Although I think staying in hotels with buffet breakfasts and spa services is great, traveling with camping gear is a cool alternative. This type of travel can be exhausting at first. But the relaxation effect is equally amazing. When you camp by a lake, in the mountains or by a river, you experience direct contact with the earth, the grass, the sky and the trees. You are literally one with nature. When camping, you are independent of fixed accommodations and can move freely. You can wake up in a new place every day and experience new adventures. There are no fixed plans or times - you can decide spontaneously where to go next. And the beauty of camping is that you reduce your possessions to the bare essentials and learn to get by with very little.

Another fascinating and wonderful way of relaxed travel is the vacation in the Tiny House. Here, usually no more than 6 square meters are available for sleeping, cooking and showering. The exciting trend originally comes from the USA, where more and more minimalists are leaving all their possessions behind and henceforth living in a mobile Tiny House - not just on vacation, but permanently. In this country, too, the "less is more" philosophy is gaining in importance. Rents are becoming unaffordable, consumption is being questioned and a decluttering wave is sweeping the country! As you know, I'm also a big proponent of minimalism because it allows me to have exactly this vacation feeling in my everyday life.

A minimalist lifestyle provides instant relaxation by eliminating unnecessary items, excess furniture, piles of clothes and tedious chores. Those who keep their household minimalist have less work to do, gaining valuable time for relaxation and leisure. A vacation in a Tiny House would be a wonderful opportunity to experience and get a taste of life as a minimalist. It is a unique experience that teaches us how little we really need to be happy and content.

# Addresses for vacations in the Tiny House

Here are some addresses (in Germany and Austria) for vacations in a small space:

## Tiny House Village

In the picturesque Fichtelgebirge mountains, more precisely in Mehlmeisel between Bayreuth and Marktredwitz, the Tiny House Village stands on a spacious site of 17,000 square meters. The foundation of the village goes back to the dedicated young couple Steffi and Phillip. In the summer of 2017, the Tiny House Village opened and three years later it received official approval for a permanent development. Several Tiny Houses are available for rent and more are being added all the time. In addition, the village offers the possibility of trial living and pitches for your own (brought) cottages. Here you can spend a relaxing vacation and experience the freedom of minimalist living first hand.

Mehr Infos gibt's unter www.tinyhousevillage.de

## Tiny House Rheinau

In Mühlbach near Rheinau, a small town in Baden-Württemberg between Baden-Baden, Kehl and Strasbourg, Tiny Houses of various sizes can be rented. The charming little houses are located in the immediate vicinity of gardens and hiking trails that can be explored directly, as those responsible assure us. It should be noted, however, that the houses can only be reached by car, as public transport in the region is not particularly well developed.

Thus the journey without passenger car becomes a small adventure. On site, there is the possibility of test living and individual consultation. There are several pitches to choose from, starting at 300 euros per month. In order to become fair the rising demand, constantly new pitches are opened. On the website of the provider, interested parties can also find useful information on topics such as building application, financing options, transport and other accessories related to the Tiny House. All the relevant information can be obtained here to make the most of the Tiny House experience.

Mehr Infos dazu auf www.tiny-house-rheinau.de

## More than Tiny Housing - the self-sufficient Wohnwagon project

Wohnwagon is one of the pioneers of the self-sufficient Tiny House movement in Europe. In the towns of Traismauer, Rechberg and Gutenstein (Austria), as well as in Oberscheiding and Niederhausen (Germany), interested parties can live in a Tiny House on a trial basis. An overnight stay costs from 140 euros for two people. Wohnwagon offers the opportunity to experience the minimalist lifestyle in the Tiny Houses for a limited period of time and discover the benefits of self-sufficient and sustainable living. In addition, the Wohnwagon website serves as a comprehensive source of information on all topics related to self-sufficient living.

Mehr Infos zu Wohnwagon auf: www.wohnwagon.at

## Further information

Who looks for still a "room in the countryside" and only little luggage brings, becomes on different Internet sides fündig: for example with www.Camp-Hotel.com, https://tinyhouse-mieten.com/, https://greentinyhouses.com/standorte or also with https://tiny-houses.de/. They all offer a large selection of accommodations from Denmark to Italy. To the selection classical Tiny Houses, construction vehicles, camping huts, Jurten, circus wagons, safari tents or caravans stand. Simply select the desired accommodation on the website, click on the desired location on the map and contact the provider directly. There one receives further information about the reservation.

The examples show: You don't have to go far afield to experience a great vacation, and you certainly don't have to go on a typical (package) vacation

# Conclusion

For many people, traveling and discovering the world is certainly an enriching experience. When traveling, one comes into contact with other cultures, gets to know the everyday life and living conditions of other people, and benefits from ancient knowledge, new ways of thinking, rich traditions, and wonderful personalities. But I hope that with this book I could show that it is not necessary to find all this also in everyday life.

Happiness, fulfillment, but also encounters and surprises do not necessarily have to be sought in faraway places. My personal "vacation feeling" unfolds here and now, right on my doorstep. I don't need any legitimation over 12,000 kilometers, no visa, no suitcase and no passport. My vacation takes place in my immediate surroundings, in leisure time, in exchanges and in the beautiful moments that keep happening. It is up to us to recognize and appreciate the wonderful and beautiful in everyday life!

I am firmly convinced that you can design your life so that it always feels like a vacation. It starts with the decor of your home, shows up in your hobbies and in the free time you gain when you change just a few simple things in your life (keyword: minimalism). And the beauty of it is that this vacation never stops! You always travel light. I think that's very important, because you shouldn't have to put off the nice things, wait until the next weekend, the next vacation or even retirement to finally relax or pursue your interests.

It's not about experiencing as much as possible in your free time. Rather, it is about organizing everyday life in such a way that it is not dominated by work and demands constant performance. It's much more important to have a good time, regardless of geographic location or distance. It's all about the here and now, about what brings joy, contributes to relaxation and evokes positive feelings - preferably within your own four walls, in your own home. In this book, I have tried to give some examples of this.

I hope I was able to inspire you a little to organize your everyday life in such a way that it feels a little like a vacation. Of course, you can still plan your (annual) vacation, pack your bags and lie down on the beach for a few weeks. If you're drawn to faraway places, go for it and don't let anyone stop you.

But don't close your eyes to the beautiful moments that happen every day at your home and right in front of you: Encounters with inspiring people that make you laugh, give you goosebumps and make your heart beat faster. Regional places whose beauty takes your breath away and good conversations that last deep into the night and change your life. Be open to experiences that make you grow, that push you to your limits (and beyond), also try regional products that have just as much love, effort and heart in them and find the peace that exists nowhere else but with you.

If you don't have these experiences in your everyday life, then where? Look for them in yourself first, figure out where you're most likely to find them, and make your home a place where you love to be.

I wish you a good trip, at home and everywhere!

# More book recommendations

*Away & Aware: A Field Guide to Mindful Travel* by Sara Clemence (2018).

*The Book of Idle Pleasures* by Dan Kieran and Tom Hodgkinson (2015).

*How to be free* by Tom Hodgkinson (2007).

*Staycation Challenge: How to Gataway While Staying at Home and Discover Local Treasures* by Helen Brahms (2023).

*Goodby, Things: On Minimalist Living* by Fumio Sasaki (2017).

*The Hidden Life of Trees* by Peter Wohlleben (2017).

*You Are Here: Discovering the Magic of the Present Moment* by Thich Nhat Hanh (2010).

*The Art of Travel* by Alain de Botton (2003).

*All You Need is Less* (German Edition) by Niko Paech and Manfred Folkers (2020).

*The Staycation: The Perfect Romantic Escape with the Bestselling Author of the Cornish Cream Tea Series* by Cressida McLaughlin (2022).

*All You Need is Rest: Refresh Your Well-Being With the Power of Rest and Sleep* by Mita Mistry (2023).

*The Great British Staycation Activity Book* by Rachel Dixon and Claire Sunders (2021).

*Nomad at Home: Designing the Home more Traveled* by Hilary Robertson (2022).

*Still: The Slow Home* by Natalie Walton (2020).

*My Body, My Home: A Radical Guide to Resilience and Belonging* by Victoria Emanuela and Caitlin Metz (2020).

# The Heidelbergerin

## How the Young Heidelberg Woman Lives, Laughs, and Loves

The Heidelbergerin - is a magnificent book that takes us on a journey into the fascinating world of the city of Heidelberg and tells us the stories of its unique residents.

*"The typical Heidelbergerin is [...] in love with life, she loves the Old Town and the Neckar. In this book, you will not only learn about the mindset of the Heidelbergerin but also discover a wealth of information about Germany's oldest university town."* (Reader's review)

Allow yourself to be swept away into the vibrant tapestry of the Heidelbergerin's world. Get to know us and fall in love with the city!"

ISBN: 9783752659610

# About the author

Regina used to travel a lot. "Because it was part of life and because that´s what people do," she says. But the real (life) journey began with her studies in the social sciences and humanities - not only because she studied the phenomenon of tourism from a cultural and critical perspective, but also because it was about larger questions of life and "I began to explore my inner treasure".

Of course, during this time she also questioned the meaning of travel and the promises associated with it. But it wasn't until  after her studies, when she moved around Germany several times for work-related reasons and got to know different federal states of Germany, cities and people, that the author, cultural scientist and communications manager realised that she had long been on the road and no longer needed much to be happy. Minimalism played a big part in this, of course! "The more I focused on the beautiful things in everyday life, the less I was drawn to faraway places," she quickly realised. She does Holistay, 365 days a year.

Today, Regina owns around 300 things, has a great job and still has plenty of free time! From the minimalist's point of view, everyday life is always an exciting journey, an island of relaxation, a sea of sensory experiences - with light luggage, of course.